FRAME INNOVATION

FRAME INNOVATION

CREATE *NEW THINKING* BY DESIGN

KEES DORST

The MIT Press
Cambridge, Massachusetts
London, England

First MIT Press paperback edition, 2024

This book was set in PT Serif and Museo Sans by The MIT Press. Printed and bound in the United States of America.

Library of Congress Cataloging-in-Publication Data
Dorst, Kees.
Frame innovation : create new thinking by design / Kees Dorst.
pages cm. — (Design thinking, design theory)
Includes bibliographical references and index.
ISBN 978-0-262-32431-1 (hardcover : alk. paper), 978-0-262-55096-3 (pb.)
1. Industrial design—Methodology. I. Title.
TS171.D667 2015
745.2—dc23
2014027047

10   9   8   7

CONTENTS

Series Foreword   vii
Acknowledgments   xiii
Preface   xv

1   CHALLENGES   1
We are not solving our problems anymore   1
The challenges   9
Moving forward   18

2   PIONEERS   23
The Young Designers foundation   23
The Designing Out Crime center   30
Learning from the pioneers   37

3   LESSONS FROM DESIGN   41
Four questions about design   41
An anatomy of design practices   55
Five lessons from design   59

4   THE FRAME CREATION MODEL   73
Frame creation   73
Case studies   80
First remarks   97

5   THE PRINCIPLES AND PRACTICES OF FRAME CREATION   99
    The principles of frame creation   99
    Frame creation practices   109

6   THE OPEN, COMPLEX, DYNAMIC, AND NETWORKED
    ORGANIZATION   121
    Driving innovation   121
    Toward frame innovation   126

7   THE THREE CHALLENGES OF FRAME INNOVATION   133
    Seeing differently   134
    Thinking differently   135
    Doing differently   143

8   THE ART OF FRAME INNOVATION   151
    Making it happen   151
    Path to action   171

    Appendix 1   An Expert Designer at Work   177
    Appendix 2   Is Design "Searching" or "Learning"?   183
    Appendix 3   More Research Is Needed   187
    Appendix 4   Inspiration   189
    References   193
    Index   201

SERIES FOREWORD

As professions go, design is relatively young. The practice of design predates professions. In fact, the practice of design—making things to serve a useful goal, making tools—predates the human race. Making tools is one of the attributes that made us human in the first place.

Design, in the most generic sense of the word, began over 2.5 million years ago when *Homo habilis* manufactured the first tools. Human beings were designing well before we began to walk upright. Four hundred thousand years ago, we began to manufacture spears. By forty thousand years ago, we had moved up to specialized tools.

Urban design and architecture came along ten thousand years ago in Mesopotamia. Interior architecture and furniture design probably emerged with them. It was another five thousand years before graphic design and typography got their start in Sumer with the development of cuneiform. After that, things picked up speed.

All goods and services are designed. The urge to design—to consider a situation, imagine a better situation, and act to create that improved situation—goes back to our prehuman ancestors. Making tools helped us to become what we are—design helped to make us human.

Today, the word "design" means many things. The common factor linking them is service, and designers are engaged in a service profession in which the results of their work meet human needs.

Design is first of all a process. The word "design" entered the English language in the sixteenth century as a verb, with the first written citation of the verb dated to the year 1548. *Merriam-Webster's Collegiate Dictionary* defines the verb "design" as "to conceive and plan out in the mind; to have as a specific purpose; to devise for a specific function or end." Related to these definitions is the act of drawing, with an emphasis on the nature of the drawing as a plan or map, as well as "to draw plans for; to create, fashion, execute, or construct according to plan."

Half a century later, the word began to be used as a noun, with the first cited use of the noun "design" occurring in 1588. *Merriam-Webster's* defines the noun as "a particular purpose held in view by an individual or group; deliberate, purposive planning; a mental project or scheme in which means to an end are laid down." Here, too, purpose and planning toward desired outcomes are central. Among these are "a preliminary sketch or outline showing the main features of something to be executed; an underlying scheme that governs functioning, developing or unfolding; a plan or protocol for carrying out or accomplishing something; the arrangement of elements or details in a product or work of art." Today, we design large, complex process, systems, and services, and we design organizations and structures to produce them. Design has changed considerably since our remote ancestors made the first stone tools.

At a highly abstract level, Herbert Simon's definition covers nearly all imaginable instances of design. To design, Simon writes, is to "[devise] courses of action aimed at changing existing situations into preferred ones" (*The Sciences of the Artificial*, 2nd ed., 1982, p. 129). Design, properly defined, is the entire process across the full range of domains required for any given outcome.

But the design process is always more than a general, abstract way of working. Design takes concrete form in the work of the service professions that meet human needs, a broad range of making and planning disciplines. These include industrial design, graphic design, textile design, furniture design, information design, process design, product design, interaction design, transportation design, educational design, systems design, urban design, design leadership, and design management, as well as architecture, engineering, information technology, and computer science.

These fields focus on different subjects and objects. They have distinct traditions, methods, and vocabularies, used and put into practice by distinct and often dissimilar professional groups. Although the traditions dividing these groups are distinct, common boundaries sometimes form a border. Where this happens, they serve as meeting points where common concerns build bridges. Today, ten challenges uniting the design professions form such a set of common concerns.

Three performance challenges, four substantive challenges, and three contextual challenges bind the design disciplines and professions together as a common field. The performance challenges arise because all design professions

1. act on the physical world,
2. address human needs, and
3. generate the built environment.

In the past, these common attributes were not sufficient to transcend the boundaries of tradition. Today, objective changes in the larger world give rise to four substantive challenges that are driving convergence in design practice and research. These substantive challenges are

1. increasingly ambiguous boundaries between artifacts, structure, and process;
2. increasingly large-scale social, economic, and industrial frames;
3. an increasingly complex environment of needs, requirements, and constraints; and
4. information content that often exceeds the value of the physical substance.

These challenges require new frameworks of theory and research to address contemporary problem areas while solving specific cases and problems. In professional design practice, we often find that solving design problems requires interdisciplinary teams with a transdisciplinary focus. Fifty years ago, a sole practitioner and an assistant or two might have solved most design problems; today, we need groups of people with skills across several disciplines, and the additional skills that enable professionals to work with, listen to, and learn from each other as they solve problems.

Three contextual challenges define the nature of many design problems today. While many design problems function at a simpler level, these issues affect many of the major design problems that challenge us, and these challenges also affect simple design problems linked to complex social, mechanical, or technical systems. These issues are

1. a complex environment in which many projects or products cross the boundaries of several organizations and stakeholder, producer, and user groups;
2. projects or products that must meet the expectations of many organizations, stakeholders, producers, and users; and
3. demands at every level of production, distribution, reception, and control.

These ten challenges require a qualitatively different approach to professional design practice than was the case in earlier times. Past environments were simpler, and made simpler demands. Individual experience and personal development were sufficient for depth and substance in professional practice. While experience and development are still necessary, they are no longer sufficient. Most of today's design challenges require analytic and synthetic planning skills that cannot be developed through practice alone.

Professional design practice today involves advanced knowledge. This knowledge is not solely a higher level of professional practice; it is also a qualitatively different form of professional practice that emerges in response to the demands of the information society and the knowledge economy to which it gives rise.

In a recent essay, Donald Norman (2010) challenges the premises and practices of the design profession. In the past, designers operated on the belief that talent and a willingness to jump into problems with both feet gave them an edge in solving problems. Norman writes:

In the early days of industrial design, the work was primarily focused upon physical products. Today, however, designers work on organizational structure and social problems, on interaction, service, and experience design. Many problems involve complex social and political issues. As a result, designers have become applied behavioral scientists, but they are woefully undereducated for the task. Designers often fail to understand the complexity of the issues and the depth of knowledge already known. They claim that fresh eyes can produce novel solutions, but then they wonder why these solutions are seldom implemented, or if implemented, why they fail. Fresh eyes can indeed produce insightful results, but the eyes must also be educated and knowledgeable. Designers often lack the requisite understanding. Design schools do not train students about these complex issues, about the interlocking complexities of human and social behavior, about the behavioral sciences, technology, and business. There is little or no training in science, the scientific method, and experimental design.

This is not industrial design in the sense of designing products, but industry-related design, design as thought and action for solving problems and imagining new futures. This new MIT Press series of books emphasizes strategic design to create value through innovative products and services, and it emphasizes design as service through rigorous creativity, critical inquiry, and an ethics of respectful design. This rests on a sense of understanding, empathy, and appreciation for people, for nature, and for the world we shape through design. Our goal as editors is to develop a series of vital conversations that help designers and researchers to serve business, industry, and the public sector for positive social and economic outcomes.

We will present books that bring a new sense of inquiry to design, helping to shape a more reflective and stable design discipline able to support a stronger profession grounded in empirical research, generative concepts, and the solid theory that gives rise to what W. Edwards Deming (1993) described as profound knowledge. For Deming, a physicist, engineer, and designer, profound knowledge comprised systems thinking and the understanding of processes embedded in systems, an understanding of variation and the tools we need to understand variation, a theory of knowledge, and a foundation in human psychology. This is the beginning of "deep design"—the union of deep practice with robust intellectual inquiry.

A series on design thinking and theory faces the same challenges that we face as a profession. On one level, design is a general human process that we use to understand and to shape our world. Nevertheless, we cannot address this process or the world in its general, abstract form. Rather, we meet the challenges of design in specific challenges, addressing problems or ideas in a situated context. The challenges we face as designers today are as diverse as the problems clients bring us. We are involved in design for economic anchors, economic continuity, and economic growth. We design for urban needs and rural needs, for social development and creative communities. We are involved with environmental sustainability and economic policy, agriculture, competitive crafts for export, and competitive products and brands for microenterprises. We develop new products for bottom-of-pyramid markets and redevelop old products for mature or wealthy markets. Within the framework of design, we are also challenged to design for extreme situations, for biotech, nanotech, and new materials, and to design for social business, as well as to meet conceptual challenges for worlds that do not yet exist, such as the world beyond the Kurzweil singularity—and for new visions of the world that does exist.

The Design Thinking, Design Theory series from the MIT Press will explore these issues and more—meeting them, examining them, and helping designers to address them.

Join us in this journey.

Ken Friedman and Erik Stolterman
Editors, Design Thinking, Design Theory Series

ACKNOWLEDGMENTS

This book is the culmination of many years of design practice and design research, in close collaboration with many friends and colleagues. In my career I have been very fortunate to have met outstanding designers, design researchers, and design educators, and to have had the opportunity to work with them on the common quest for understanding design and developing the field. I am very grateful for their generosity, guidance, help, and friendship.

These acknowledgments include colleagues from TU Delft (Jan, Nigel, Norbert, Henri, Peter, Frido, Rianne, Remko, Rens, Paul, Pieter, and many others), TU Eindhoven (Aarnout, Jeu, Ilse, Christelle, Ad, Vera, Anthonie, Lambèr, Wybo, and again many others), and the dear colleagues that have welcomed me at UTS (Douglas, Sue, Desley, Jaqui, Louise, Hael, Attila, ...). The Young Designers foundation has been a constant source of inspiration for over twenty years, thanks to Peik, Titia, Dennis, and the many designers I met through them. Particular thanks should go to my current colleagues at the Design Innovation research center in Sydney. I am grateful for the support the Designing Out Crime center has received from my universities—the University of Technology, Sydney, and Eindhoven University of Technology—and from the New South Wales Department of Justice, Police and Attorney General, as well as from numerous project partners and students who have collaborated with us over the years. A special thanks should go to people who have been particularly important—instrumental, I should say—in the development of the frame creation approach: Peik Suyling, Dick Rijken, Douglas Tomkin, and Willem Knoop. Through many inspiring conversations, they have nurtured the thoughts that have slowly formed into the approaches and models that have now landed on these pages. The Dru yoga community has been an important source of sustenance and inspiration over the years (thank you, Franklin, Andrew, and everybody).

I would like to thank Phyllis Crabill for correcting my English, Claudy te Brake for great work on the figures, and the MIT Press editorial team for their professionalism and support. Ken Friedman, thank you so much for your encouragement in the writing process. And to end on a personal note: Paulien, my partner, my heartfelt thanks to you—for your patience and for our life together. This one is for you.

PREFACE

We are living in unusual times. Every day we are challenged to navigate an increasingly complex and dynamic world. This is true not only for us as individuals, in our private and professional lives, but also for the organizations we create and are part of. Public organizations and companies alike are learning the hard way that the problems before us now cannot be resolved in the way we approached problems in the past. But if the old ways do not work anymore, what do we do now? How can we create progress and deal with the new challenges that the world is putting before us?

As an answer to this question, this book introduces a fascinating new practice for creating original approaches to really hard problems. Frame creation is a deep and thoughtful approach for achieving radical innovation that was originally developed in the practices of expert designers. These expert designers have always been known for "solving the unsolvable," creating new solutions where others see none, and for finding new opportunities where others see only problems. But what, then, is their secret? They have a special approach to problems, called "frame creation." In this book, the frame creation approach is introduced, investigated, and then modeled so that it can be used by professionals in other fields, beyond the designing disciplines.

The book is organized as follows: first, we will need to explore the nature of today's problems, and understand what makes these problems so hard to solve (chapter 1). Learning from the practices of pioneering organizations (chapter 2) and more than fifty years of design research (chapter 3), the book builds up to a nine-step model of the frame creation process (chapter 4). The principles and practices behind these steps are clarified (chapter 5), and then the focus swerves to implementation of the frame creation approach, as tools and methods for frame innovators are formulated (chapters 6, 7, and 8). Rather than constituting a straight how-to manual for frame innovation, these tools and methods together could be compared to a do-it-yourself guide: a deep understanding of the principles and practices of frame creation will help the practitioner to develop his or her own approach to achieving radical innovation.

This book can be read in several ways. Chapter 4 contains the core model of the frame creation approach, and the nineteen case studies illustrate its use in a lively, situated, and pragmatic manner. The broader text creates a much deeper understanding of the "why" and "how," and explains how frame creation practice can radically extend our current approaches for creating innovation.

Over the years of studying designers and experimenting with frame creation, I have become convinced that this is an immensely valuable new approach to resolving problems, and create the *new thinking* that is sorely needed to deal with the newly open, complex, dynamic, and networked nature of today's world.

Kees Dorst
Sydney and Eindhoven, 2014

1 CHALLENGES

WE ARE NOT SOLVING OUR PROBLEMS ANYMORE

Look at the news this morning. If we put aside the inevitable natural disasters and the usual gossip, what stares us in the face is an endless succession of reports showing us how much trouble we have dealing with the complex issues of contemporary life. There seems to be no way out. Companies and government organizations alike are swept up in a comedy of errors, and a world of missed opportunities lies mute in the background. Sociologist Hans Boutellier has captured our current predicament well:

In today's world we have difficulty formulating grand comforting ideas. We hear a cacophony of voices and opinions, see rage and frustration, and observe a lot of ad hoc policy and tentative management. There is a lot of fumbling around without a guiding concept. ... A great deal of tinkering and muddling goes on within politics, educational institutions, the business community, retailers, the self-employed. ... If nobody knows the answer, then we choose what seems to be "best": good practices, effective interventions, evidence-based policy. We formulate a politics of risk management and crisis management. ... We let ourselves be guided by effectiveness and efficiency, preferably demonstrated by performance indicators, guided by supervision and control. (Boutellier 2013)

This is not because we are particularly dumb or inept, but because we are collectively being tripped up by today's problems. As I argue in this book, this difficulty is the result of the emergence of a radically new species of problem: problems that are so open, complex, dynamic, and networked that they seem impervious to solution. What all the news stories show us is that it makes no sense to keep trying to tackle these problems the way we used to. The trusted routines just don't work anymore. These new types of problems require a radically different response.

In searching for alternative ways to tackle these open, complex, dynamic, and networked problems, leading innovators in different fields have increasingly been turning to "design" for help. These individuals, companies, institutions, and governments are interested in design because expert designers deal with the new types of problems in their professional field without too much trouble. Under the flag of "design thinking," businesses and business schools are seeking inspiration from design-based case studies (Brown 2009; Verganti 2009; Carlopio 2010; Plattner, Meinel, and Weinberg 2009). Yet recent experience has shown that it is not easy to effectively transpose these lessons from design into other domains. The application of some cool design tricks and techniques, although liberating and inspiring, doesn't often lead to the results we really need. I will argue that this is because the interest in "design thinking" mostly focuses on the designer's abilities in generating solutions, rather than on the key ability of expert designers to create new approaches to problem situations ("framing"). The creation of new "frames" to approach problem situations is the key and special element of designers' problem-solving practices (Whitbeck 1998). While this framing of problems is a universal human ability (Gardner 1983, 2006), and thus cannot be claimed to be special to the design professions, it is particularly important (indeed, central) to the design professions. We will find that expert design practitioners have developed unique, sophisticated multilayered practices for creating new frames. After taking a very close look at the way these design practices work, this book will use these professional practices as the basis for developing an alternative to conventional problem-solving methods. Nineteen case studies will show how these design-based practices and strategies for frame creation can be extremely valuable for dealing with open, complex, dynamic, and networked problems in a broad range of domains. We will then explore how these practices can be introduced and implemented into organizations to achieve frame innovation.

The fresh practices that will be presented in this book are based on lessons learned from studying the activities of top designers, and build on the very detailed and subtle understanding of design that has emerged from over fifty years of design research. This research is a veritable treasure trove of approaches and insights. In creating the vital link between top-end design practice and conventional problem-solving, we will wander into philosophical territory every now and then—because the issues we are seeking to resolve turn out to be quite fundamental. But in the end this book is written for practitioners, it is about practices, and it is always fundamentally practical in nature. It was written because we need to extend our repertoire of problem-solving practices to deal with the complex, networked world we have created for ourselves. We do not have a moment to lose.

To begin, let's try to understand the nature of the problematic situations we find ourselves in by looking at three case histories from widely different domains.

CASE 1
The train to nowhere:
On decision-making about public infrastructure

For years, a high-speed train link was being planned in Holland, a small and densely populated European country. This link would connect major cities like Rotterdam and Amsterdam to the pan-European high-speed train network that has been built over the last thirty years. The link was seen as strategically important for economic, social, and cultural reasons. Not joining the network would leave Holland relatively isolated—geographically, the country is just north of the main population centers of the European Union. The proud and sophisticated Dutch government apparatus braced itself for a long and difficult planning process: the adverse consequences for thousands of people living and working along the proposed train route were only too easy to imagine. Who would welcome the thought of a 450-ton steel monster racing through their backyard at 300 km/hour, every ten minutes or so? The impact of noise, ruined views, vibration, and property devaluation is potentially huge. In a more hierarchical country (with a higher "power distance" [Hofstede 1997, 2001]) or in a less crowded country, the planning of a new train link might not be a problem. But in this case it was. Impact studies were made, and years were spent in elaborate community consultation procedures. Forums were created so that everyone could have his or her say, all according to best practice in democratic government. All this was done in the belief that through these discussions rationality would prevail, and a consensus could be reached. But every time one of the proposed routes took the lead, local councils and citizen groups commissioned their own studies to show that the government's research was incomplete, or plainly wrong. While the tabled arguments were often plausible, the motivation behind them was, of course, the classic NIMBY: "Not In My Back Yard." The confusion that ensued from this proliferation of studies was exacerbated by the fact that by this time (the mid-nineties) the Internet was coming of age and the number of stakeholders involved in these processes skyrocketed: apart from the obvious institutional stakeholders like the railway company, the main airport, or the local councils, the project was besieged by a wild variety of environmental groups, NGOs, and lobbying groups of concerned citizens expressing their views and gathering support. Interest groups started to come up with their own proposals for where to situate the train line, and launched those schemes in the press complete with "independent" studies to support their merit. In a desperate effort to reach a consensus, the government felt duty-bound to consider every new alternative. It kept commissioning extra studies to evaluate these proposals, thus dragging out the decision process even more. The local interest groups were supported by the local councils, who were getting caught between the interests of the state and the need to represent the views of their angry citizens. The councils of the towns and cities along the proposed routes sought to resolve this paradox by explaining that while they didn't want the noise, they could live with it if they were compensated with the economic benefits of their own station on the train line (a compromise that, unfortunately, does not make sense for a high-speed train).

The planning process dragged on for fifteen years, with no conclusion in sight (Priemus 2009). Meanwhile, the people living and working along the proposed routes were becoming traumatized by the constant uncertainty caused by this prolonged decision process. In the end, even the press got tired of it. Voices of those wanting to just forget the whole project were getting louder and louder: not because the train link was a bad idea, for there was general consensus that the country could ill afford *not* to be connected to the European network, but because no agreement could be reached on the route. After fifteen years of planning and deliberation, this process ground to a halt, collapsing under the weight of the paradoxes in the problem situation and the dilemmas presented by the different solutions. It could have remained stuck forever ... but, in the end, the deadlock was broken by the election of a new government, which included parties that had pledged to forge ahead with the project.

By that time, two dominant trajectories for the rail link had emerged, the first of which more or less followed a straight line from the border to its terminus in Amsterdam. This proposal, created by the government planning office, was the one the ministry had been pushing all along. The second proposal was created by an ex–civil servant and cleverly minimized the impact of the new train line by linking its trajectory to the existing freeway network at the cost of just a couple of minutes in extra travel time. In the end, the government planning office's route was chosen, with the addition of a major tunnel to minimize the impact on a sensitive environmental area on the route. The decision was reached by some old-fashioned political power plays, and the outcome was only vaguely related to reality. The politicians were locked in groupthink, and did not realize that this compromise was both unfortunate in its impact and spectacularly expensive compared to both original plans (Priemus 2009).

Although this is an example of public problem-solving at its very worst, it is by no means an exceptional story. This type of decision-making happens everywhere, all the time—just look at the news ... This example had an interesting sequel: once the bulldozers were rolling through the landscape and the concrete was being poured, Parliament in its wisdom passed a motion to investigate and evaluate the decision process of the high-speed train project, as it was deemed to be clearly flawed. Resorting to political arm-twisting around such an important issue which touched the lives of so many people is highly regrettable. The parliamentary inquiry filed its report a year later, with its main recommendation being that more research should have been done on the various plans under consideration. Yet if we retrace the history of the project, we can only conclude that more research would not have helped at all. One can only surmise that this recommendation was caused by the foolhardy belief that rationality would then prevail. But that is not the issue: conventional problem-solving had reached the end of its tether, which is why the planning process had ground to a halt. The parliamentary inquiry's recommendation for more research demonstrates their complete inability to even imagine a different kind of problem-solving practice. We will get back to this case study at the end of this book (in chapter 8), and will demonstrate that there is a viable way to approach this problem. The journey to get there starts with the realization that *this problem is actually not about the train.*

CASE 2
The dematerialization of products:
On navigating the postindustrial economy

We live in an age in which the industrial society, based on manufacturing physical goods and selling them to consumers, is giving way to a society in which information and services are much more important. This transformation necessitates a huge shift for many organizations that have grown up and thrived in the industrial age—they are used to dealing with change in terms of advances in technology and shifts in market preference, but nothing has prepared them for the fundamental challenges that confront them now. As an example, let's look at Bang and Olufsen, a world-renowned Danish company that produces high-end audio equipment. Only a few years ago, the future of this company looked very bright. The company had been well known for over thirty years as the producer of an iconic range of very austere, modernist audio equipment. The identity of the company was strongly associated with these high-quality "design classics" (Dickson 2006). However, to hold this enviable market position, the company could never rest on its laurels: continuous innovation was needed to stay at the forefront of developments in audio technology, and to cleverly incorporate these cutting-edge technologies into new products that would harmonize with the company's signature modernist aesthetic. The company mastered this extremely subtle design game successfully. But the absolute test of Bang and Olufsen's problem-solving ability came when the profitable high end of the consumer market quite suddenly abandoned the traditional concept of a "sound system" as a product that is placed in a living room. These high-end consumers started buying audio systems that are built into the structure of the house itself (*domotica*, or "home automation") and controlled by a remote—thus hiding the source of all that music from view. The disappearance of the sound system as an identifiable product was, of course, a huge problem for a company that prides itself on the production of beautiful objects. As a response, Bang and Olufsen set out to develop a new way of expressing the core qualities of its material products in a nonmaterial way. It experimented with the creation of interface devices and interface scenarios that would hold the same subtle qualities as their classic products. But as they were performing this pioneering R&D work, another change hit the market. The ubiquitous presence of mobile technology and the Internet paved the way for the integration of music players into computers, tablets, and smartphones. Music became something that was downloaded or bought online, shared socially, and consumed casually on mobile devices. This reframing of the meaning of music in people's lives meant that audio quality became less of a concern to most users, aside from a small select group of connoisseurs. Bang and Olufsen found that it needed to shift its value proposition again, and found that its sophisticated skills, knowledge, and practices were exquisitely honed to a world that had changed beyond recognition (see also the Bang and Olufsen case study in

Verganti 2009). We will return to this case study later; new approaches become possible once one realizes that *this problem requires a complete redefinition of "quality," away from conventional notions of (product) aesthetics.*

The passing of the structures and systems of the industrial age and the rise of a networked society have resulted in open, complex, dynamic, and networked challenges that can only be successfully met by organizations that are ready to become open, complex, and networked themselves. The advent of a postindustrial age has a profound effect on the way our economies and societies work—nothing really stays the same. For a manufacturing company like Bang and Olufsen, this shift has led their products to disappear into service networks. Further down the chain, the retail outlets that were the podium on which companies in the industrial economy could express the special qualities of their products are also under pressure, as the Internet is a serious competitor as a point of sale. It is as if history is repeating itself: where the increasing availability of private cars diminished the proximity value of the old neighborhood shop in favor of shopping malls and city centers, the Internet now creates a new situation in which the product monopoly of the shopping mall in turn is challenged. People still visit shops to see the products that they are interested in, but they might decide to buy later and order the items online. As we will see in case study 12 (chapter 4), the rise of the Internet requires a radical rethinking both of the value of products and of the shop as a physical outlet where they can be bought.

CASE 3
Carrying the weight of the world:
On the many challenges of social housing

Early social housing projects in the West were part of a movement to clear the nineteenth-century slums that housed the workers of the industrial revolution. These efforts were redoubled in face of the rapidly rising population after the Second World War, peaking in the 1960s and 1970s. This was not a morally neutral endeavor: councils and social housing associations were as patronizing as they were well-meaning, setting out to change the way "those people" lived by providing a very specific infrastructure. These "estates" were utopian in a way, the carriers of high ideals—yet they were not built on a deep understanding of the everyday life of the people they were to house (after all, the idealists were planning to change that). The overwhelming focus was on speed and scale. Whole new towns were rolled out in the landscape outside of our old cities in a forbidding and anonymizing modernist architecture. They were often very cheaply built, with the new techniques of precast concrete slabs allowing quick assembly on site. Some of the high-rises are system building at its worst. After an optimistic, bright and sunny start, these estates began to get run down. The working class, which made up the vast majority of the population on these estates, was particularly vulnerable to changes in society in the 1970s and 1980s as many Western economies moved away from resource industries like mining and eventually also from manufacturing toward a service economy. This brave new postindustrial world required a completely different skillset from its workers. People who were never rich to begin with found themselves on a downward slope, without any means of reversing the steady decline (Bourdieu et al. 1999). At the same time, the boom in property prices caused city life to become increasingly expensive. The housing estates were often the cheapest places to live within this new ecosystem, and consequently they attracted an influx of people who, through nature or nurture, could not connect to the new economy—bringing mental issues, poverty, drugs, and crime into these areas. Bourdieu's chilling description of the plight of people in a region in the south of France where new management practices and a general economic shift led to decreasing employment in a once-thriving industrial area makes for extremely depressing reading. Social suffering becomes entrenched as it is passed on from generation to generation. Immigrant workers (legal and illegal) coming into these areas often raised a new generation growing up in poverty, with a general frustration at the lack of opportunities easily leading to lethargy and a harsh, cynical street culture.

In many estates crime surges, creating an even grimmer situation (Hanley 2007). The incredibly complex network of factors conspiring together to create these problematic situations makes them almost impervious to change. The buildings themselves become very visible symbols of failure, as "slums in the sky." The stigma that became associated with them reduces the life opportunities of their inhabitants even further. Ill-conceived public spaces create a soulless atmosphere, and the relative isolation of many estates (poor transport, poor shops, and most importantly poor schools) contribute to a downward pull on the inhabitants. Young families who can move away do so, and the people who remain are basically stuck. Polite society tends to look away from these issues, and (literally) does not want to go there. The question of what to do now rests with the social housing providers, often local councils or social housing authorities. Most of these housing authorities were originally set up as organizations to efficiently roll out large housing projects. To give them credit, many of them now support their communities of tenants with very committed networks of social workers. But their conventional problem-solving strategies still concentrate on the "bricks and mortar," and when the social problems become overwhelming, they seek physical solutions (pulling down the buildings, and starting all over). This tendency is reinforced by the media, which invariably portrays these neighborhoods as drab, gray, and menacing. But we will see later in this chapter (and in case study 15) that this requires new thinking. There are other ways to address these dauntingly complex problem situations, if we start from the realization that *this problem is not about the buildings.*

THE CHALLENGES

Now we need to spend a couple of moments on understanding these challenges better. First we will look at the nature of the kind of problem we are up against, and ask the question, "What do we actually mean when we talk about 'open, complex, dynamic, and networked problems'?" (see figure 1.1). Then we will look into what makes these problems hard to solve, identifying the counterforces in organizations that keep them from addressing these problems effectively: the five syndromes of conventional organizations.

So what do we mean when we say that these contemporary problems have an "open, complex, dynamic, and networked" nature? Point by point:

"OPEN"
An open problem is one where the system border is not clear, or where it is permeable. It is important to realize that normally when we start out solving a problem we draw a mental circle, nominating things to think about and what to leave out. Anything beyond the circle we call "context," and that will not play a part in our thinking about the problem. Yet in some cases now, we find problem situations in which it is very unclear where this circle should be drawn, where we really cannot say what can be safely excluded and ignored. Any rash

assumptions that some factor or stakeholder can be excluded may come back to haunt you later on in the problem-solving process. Problem and context seem to merge.

"COMPLEX"

A complex problem is one that consists of many elements, with numerous connections between them. These connections may themselves be interdependent, creating a system where one small local decision can lead to lots of repercussions and chain effects in other seemingly unrelated areas. These interrelationships make it very hard to *split up* the overall problem situation into smaller chunks that could be dealt with more easily (as one does in conventional problem-solving): one can never be sure that in doing so you are not severing key relations. If key relations are accidentally severed, they will need to be reestablished later in the problem-solving process, when they will present themselves as flaws in the solution or, indeed, as fresh problems. Furthermore, the very number of elements and relationships also makes it well-nigh impossible to *abstract* from a complex problem (which would be the alternative strategy to cutting up the problem). The tangle of elements and connections means that these problems basically have to be approached as a whole, in all their complexity. But how can you do so? We will see that this is an area where expert designers have some interesting strategies.

"DYNAMIC"

A dynamic problem situation changes over time, with the addition of new elements and the shifting of connections (e.g., through the shifting of priorities). These can be slow changes, driven by ponderous processes like cultural change, or lightning-quick movements driven by technological development, for instance. Some of these dynamic changes we can predict by realizing that irresolvable issues tend to generate an oscillation, the type of dynamism that is a swinging movement—especially when the feedback mechanism is slow. For example, we often see this in the management of large organizations, which tend to be forever in flux between centralization and decentralization. Both of these modalities have their pros and cons, and management tends to keep compensating for these by "reorganizing." The pendulum between centralized and decentralized management swings back and forth. One could plan for that. The wildly dynamic problem situations, of which we will encounter several in this book, are much more problematic. But as we will learn from expert designers, one can prepare for these challenges, too.

OPEN
NO BOUNDARIES
COMPLEX
MANY ELEMENTS AND RELATIONSHIPS
DYNAMIC
CHANGE OVER TIME
NETWORKED
ACROSS ORGANIZATIONS

Figure 1.1
The nature of contemporary problems.

"NETWORKED"

The networked nature of today's problem situations means that they potentially influence each other constantly—as we saw in the first case study, where the rise of the Internet confounded the government's efforts to reach consensus on the route of the railway line. What other people are doing in seemingly unrelated fields might cause an effect that severely influences your problem field and options for action. Examples abound—and we will see another example of an unexpected stakeholder influencing the issues around social housing later in this chapter.

"OPEN, COMPLEX, DYNAMIC, AND NETWORKED"

All together, these four properties of the new problem situations severely challenge the assumptions behind our conventional ways of solving problems. We will see in chapter 7 that any one of these is already enough to pull the rug out from under most conventional problem-solving strategies, and the case studies above have shown that they can be really disconcerting in combination.

These open, complex, dynamic, and networked problems just do not gel well with the assumptions behind our conventional problem-solving methods, because most of our conventional strategies were conceived to work in a reasonably isolated, static, and hierarchically ordered "miniworld." When problems appeared, we could isolate them in a separate problem arena, decompose the problem into relative simple subproblems and analyze these, create subsolutions, and then build those subsolutions together into an overall solution that satisfied all concerned. If this strategy of divide-and-solve failed, we could use the alternative strategy of exercising authority to "simplify" the problem area by overruling some parties, and force a solution that satisfied the most powerful player.

But neither of these strategies works for today's problems. We are living in a state of hyperconnectivity. Each of us has become newly connected to innumerable other people. By networking our society, we have inadvertently networked our problems, too—we have made them more open, complex, and dynamic! The enclosed miniworlds of our societies, economies, and cultures have been replaced by a tangle of relationships within complex and overlapping networks, where problems cannot be simplified by being split up (the network of relationships is too strong) and power doesn't rest in one place anymore (so overrule-and-conquer is out of the question). Moreover, problems are so intimately related to each other (and there are so many interdependencies) that they become impossible to isolate (Stacey, Griffin, and Shaw 2006; Lawson 2001). Solving problems nowadays is like trying to undo the Gordian knot in Greek mythology: whatever string you try to pull to unravel the knot, you end up in more of a jumble.

From the three case histories above, we can also learn that these peculiar open, complex, dynamic, and networked problems cannot be pinned down very easily—if at all. They are more like "problem situations" in which the issues keep shifting around, and any premature attempt to draft a problem definition can lead to suboptimal or even counterproductive solutions. Yet in conventional problem-solving, the "definition of the problem" is always the first step, and it is the solid ground on which the problem-solving practices of organizations are built. Often, organizations that do not realize the open, complex, dynamic, and networked nature of the world around them get tricked into using their established routines because the problem, as they define it for themselves, mostly looks the same as earlier problems. And indeed, the core problems themselves may not have changed much over time (after all, we have planned train lines for over 150 years; we should know how to do this)—but the problem boundaries are harder to draw, and there is a much more complex and dynamic context around the problems we are facing today. That context ultimately defines what practices will work, and which will fail.

Even organizations that fully realize the fluid nature of the world around them often feel they cannot move forward without first defining the problem. But by defining the problem, they inadvertently freeze the context too, and more often than not this is a grave mistake that will come back to haunt them as they try to implement their new solution. One of the core lessons that we will draw from the expert designers' practices that will be introduced in the next chapters is that new approaches can be developed to deal with open, complex, dynamic, and networked problem situations without prematurely fixing the problem formulation.

But before we start prescribing a "cure" that will help organizations deal with problem-solving in a different way, we first need to explore what lies behind their current conventional problem-solving practices. And we need to ask ourselves what makes these practices so resistant to change, even in the face of overwhelming evidence that they do not deliver the expected results anymore. To put it in terms of medical diagnostics, we need to get beyond the symptoms of these problem-solving breakdowns, and examine the syndromes that are at the root of it all. The examples described above illustrate a variety of degrees and kinds of "stuckness" that organizations (whether public-sector organizations or commercial companies) experience these days. Let's explore the underlying syndromes that all have in common (see figure 1.2).

"THE LONE WARRIOR"

First of all, we can observe that in all these cases the problem-solving situation was set in such a way that one major party rightly or wrongly felt that they "owned" the problem and needed to drive the problem-solving process, and they honestly believed this approach to be in everyone's best interest. In cases like these, one party seeks total control over the problem-solving process, and usually positions itself outside the problem-solving arena (everything else needs to change, but never them). While that may be a good and efficient way to work in conventional problem situations, we can see that in situations like the high-speed train problem, where other stakeholders seek to influence the solution, conflicts arise immediately. There has been no process to create a basis of trust and understanding between the lead organization and these

LONE WARRIOR

FREEZE THE WORLD

SELF-MADE BOX

RATIONAL HIGH GROUND

IDENTIFICATION

Figure 1.2
The five syndromes of conventional organizations.

interested parties to enable a genuine, effective collaboration to occur. And it is very hard for organizations to understand their own role in creating the disconnect, let alone to change their singular approach into a more collaborative one once the project is under way. Once the process has started off on the wrong foot, it is very hard to change. In the commercial world, projects that have started without an open engagement with the people they are setting out to create value for are very hard to redirect (Harkema 2012). In public-sector consultation processes, parties often dig in after an initial skirmish, and at that point the whole process shifts from dealing with the problem to discussions that focus only on "position bargaining." In all the open, complex, dynamic, and networked problem situations above, the problem-solving situation can move forward only through collaboration.

The pattern that emerges is that the lead party who had heroically shouldered too much of the problem-solving responsibility is just one step away from deep frustration. This party will see the involvement of others as "interference," and feel misunderstood and unappreciated in their implacable motivation. These are strong sentiments that easily turn into anger, and often cause them to stop listening to others altogether.

"FREEZE THE WORLD"

Conventional problem-solving processes tend to be curiously static. Apparently, conventional problem-solving requires us to stop the world, isolate the problem, and come up with a one-off solution. But in an environment that is very dynamic and open, this approach just isn't realistic: the influence of time and connectedness means that the borders around the problem situation are very permeable, and that the rules of the game keep changing over time. The presence of such a "freeze the world" practice is indicated by telltale signs like endless amounts of preliminary research and interminable working group discussions before a project is allowed to start. The problem solver tries to carefully understand the problem situation before deciding on an elegant and convincing solution. This approach is curiously nonexperimental, and underlying it is the apparent need to attain complete closure before the solution is put into action. When the problem solvers realize they have failed to contain the problem-solving situation and are swept along in a dynamic process, or "thrown" into situations (Winograd and Flores 1986, quoting Heidegger) that are not of their making, they feel they are losing control. Forced to improvise when they are unwilling or ill-equipped to do so, they might just stop in their tracks. This is called the "freeze the world" syndrome.

"THE SELF-MADE BOX"

All organizations will initially try to approach a new problem in ways that have worked in the past. This reaction is completely understandable—it is prudent to avoid the investment and hassle that always accompanies change unless it is really necessary. Even organizations that pride themselves on being innovators in their field aim to be just ahead of the others, and avoid unwarranted innovation. But in these case studies, we have seen that there is a great reluctance to change tack even when these trusted practices are clearly not delivering the desired results. The organizations seem to be trapped by their habits.

In a worst-case scenario, the organization might be holding on to its conventional practices for dear life, often not even knowing why. This grasping is accompanied by a degree of defeatism or melancholia, a nostalgia for the times when the world was still understandable, a golden age that is now long gone.

This pattern of behavior, effectively the locking down of a problem situation, leads to a deeply engrained inability of organizations to step beyond the boundaries of their earlier ways of thinking. Creativity consultants then provide workshops to help people "think outside the box"—which may help a little, but organizations often do not realize what a real change in their own practice will mean, and do not realize that the boxes they are trying to escape from are completely self-made. Later in this book we will see how design practitioners manage to escape creating these thought traps for themselves. The "self-made box" is an important syndrome because in a truly bound situation, even very mild and reasonable people can be strangely persistent, relentlessly pushing a certain problem-solving approach for lack of alternatives. They are blocking new thinking and reinforcing the patterns of the "self-made box."

"TAKING THE RATIONAL HIGH GROUND"

Deep down, all organizations that display clear signs of these first three syndromes are convinced that their way of dealing with the problem situation is completely rational, and that they couldn't have done anything else. This belief in their own rationality, and the deeply rooted conviction that there is only one rational position, can make organizations strangely inflexible in their problem-solving approach. This inflexibility persists even to the point of inducing a curious repetitiveness, where we see an organization using the same disastrous approach over and over again. The same government that planned the high-speed train link also constructed a major freight line running right through the country a couple of years later. That project displayed exactly the same dysfunctional pattern as the one before (de Vries and Bordewijk 2009). The strong pattern that emerges here goes beyond clinging to cherished assumptions or preconceptions: at its core is the conviction that the organization's problem-solving actions are completely rational and deeply self-evident. This is reminiscent of the way generals in the First World War kept ordering waves of attacks on the enemy trenches—only to have their troops mowed down time and again. Even when this sometimes happened several times a day, they persisted because they just had no other strategy to break the stalemate. Thus there is a strange correlation between the unquestioning belief in a certain type of rationality and the utter madness of continuing to apply it in situations where it clearly doesn't work.

Symptomatic behavior that accompanies this syndrome can be the repetitious use of sentences that start with "Of course ... ," exemplifying the inability to discuss other viewpoints. Such appeals to rationality and causation come with a second claim, and that is to the moral high ground of "reasonableness." This can easily result in the adoption of a nonnegotiable position in the problem-solving process and in stubborn perseverance. Attachment to the rational high ground is accompanied by an acute fear of what might lie beyond the confines of this rationality, which is often referred to in terms of anarchy and chaos. Many organizations hold on to the "rational high ground" for dear life, to avoid slipping into the quicksand where "trial and error" may be the only way forward.

"SHAPE YOUR IDENTITY AROUND ESTABLISHED PRACTICES"

Well-worn problem-solving paths become deeply entrenched in the minds of people, and indeed in the structure and procedures of an organization. They easily become a major part of what people feel is the organization's core, its identity and "culture." This culture is embodied in the organization's goals, structures, processes, espoused values, practices, and the accepted definition of "quality" within the organization. If the organization operates in a stable environment and has the time to hone its procedures to perfection, and its culture is seen to be very successful, the emotional bond of people with what they see as the unchangeable DNA of the organization can become very strong.

Persistence in holding on to an organization's practices can be seen most clearly and explicitly in what is called organizational autopoiesis, the subtle ways in which new staff members are initiated into "how we do things here" by the resident staff. Initiation starts as soon as the new person arrives (which incidentally can be frustrating to the management if they had tried to bring fresh ideas and new practices into the organization by hiring this person). This pathological identification with current practice has been described as an organization's culture becoming "self-sealing" (Argyris 2000), and it is the absolute death knell to any innovation. A self-sealed culture makes it extremely difficult for the staff to even think of new practices, no matter how strongly and obviously they are needed to meet changes in the external environment.

MOVING FORWARD

As Boutellier remarks (2013), complexity without direction paralyzes.

The feeling of powerlessness that permeates the case studies can be traced back to these five underlying syndromes, which will each be further explored throughout the book. But before we go on, it is important to realize that the proponents of the nineteen case studies in this book are actually all very good organizations, which have operated successfully in their respective domains for many years. The people in these organizations are highly educated, highly skilled, well-meaning, experienced, motivated, clever, and proactive. The fact that such impressive organizations find themselves staring at these new types of problems in a dumbfounded manner is what sparked the writing of this book.

And we have to realize that shifting these old ways of problem-solving is not going to be easy. The five syndromes that prevent us from addressing these open, complex, dynamic, and networked problem situations in novel ways are literally as old as humanity. This is why they are so recognizable—they are deeply rooted in us, and in our professional cultures. In fact, these patterns of thought can be chased all the way back to the big books of humanity. "Lone warriors" already populated the Bible, the Koran, and the Bhagavad-Gita. Even though the lone warrior pattern with all its heroism and dysfunctional romanticism was brilliantly mocked by Cervantes in his *Don Quixote*, the long line of archetypal lone warriors has continued, extending unabated to today's children's books and Hollywood blockbusters. Likewise, the idea that a "frozen world" is necessary to solve any problem is another assumption that permeates our stories, films, and literature—think about crime stories, for instance. The Sherlock Holmeses always discover the perpetrator from a select group of suspects that is isolated in a house, on a train, in a specific family constellation, or (nowadays) in a spaceship. The "self-made box" of received wisdom and conventional practices is often considered the very core of the culture of our societies, and eagerly reinforced by popular media. The "rational high ground" that is often implied in this claim to authority sparks another archetype: the clever outsider who runs circles around accepted behavior. These jester-like figures are consistent across time and cultures: examples range from Loki in Celtic mythology to the Tengu in Japan, and the stand-up comedian of today. But this carnival of ritualized dissent implicitly recognizes the importance of the consensus and the powers that be (Le Roy Ladurie 1979). The dark logic behind the state apparatus in Orwell's *1984* offers us a dystopic view of what the enforcement of a limited, twisted rationality can lead to. But that book becomes really chilling when the reader realizes that the logic is completely sealed within the "identity" of the society, and everybody in it. There is no escape possible from this closed totalitarian culture, and all deeds of resistance will ultimately be doomed. The self-sealing mechanism is very serious, indeed ...

Thus, there is no question that the syndromes we are dealing with here are deeply engrained, because they serve important purposes in creating stability and continuity. They cannot be "solved" or eliminated—but we will see later in this book that they can be overcome when that is needed.

Frame creation is an opportunity to approach the problems we face in novel ways, and avoid repeating the dysfunctional problem-solving practices of the past. As a first example, in the next case study the complex and deeply engrained problems of a social housing situation are approached in an original and very effective manner, bypassing all conventional problem-solving strategies.

CASE 4
Stories to connect people:
On reframing housing issues

An early project that pioneered a completely different approach to the bricks-and-mortar thinking that dominates the cultural DNA of social housing authorities took place in the late 1990s in Amsterdam. It was sparked by the pressing issues of a neighborhood that had seen a substantial influx of immigrants from Turkey and Morocco. These new communities introduced a different culture to the old area, now vibrant with "Eastern" shops and newly built mosques. In their midst still lived an aging Dutch population (Dutch families with children tended to move away from this area, to the suburbs) who were feeling more and more lost within their familiar surroundings. They perceived the neighborhood as going downhill, a feeling of unsafety that was exacerbated when some public spaces were vandalized. Everybody kept more or less to themselves, and it was clear that the influx of new people did not contribute to an inclusive social network. While there were no immediate problems, the social structure was felt to be close to collapse (De Gruijter, van Waesberge, and Boutellier 2010). From interviews, researchers learned that many of the recent (and not-so-recent) arrivals saw their existence in this cold, wet country as temporary—they intended to return to Turkey or Morocco when they were old.

This actually didn't happen at all; the first-generation immigrants stayed with their kids who had grown up in the new country. However, while these children (the second generation) grew up within the Dutch culture, the first-generation immigrants did not mentally adopt Holland as their new home, inadvertently creating enclaves where they could feel comfortable among themselves, but not connecting with broader Dutch society. This larger social drama was played out on a local scale in this particular part of the city.

Later, the Amsterdam Historic Museum coordinated a project to collect stories about this neighborhood by interviewing the older Dutch population, to give a sense of depth to the place (what could be called "a deep map" [Heat-Moon 1999]). A website was created in which these anecdotes were displayed (http://www.geheugenvanoost.nl), and was advertised locally. In the end, people from the Turkish and Moroccan communities also got involved, relating their own experiences of arriving and living in the area. When they started recounting stories about their life in the places they had come from, the project staff realized that they did not come from "Turkey" or "Morocco," but that each community was rooted in just a few specific villages in rural areas of those countries. The older Dutch population could relate to these stories of rural life—they were not that different from their own family histories one or two generations back, when their own ancestors moved to the city from the Dutch countryside. The network of stories expressed many more common values than anyone could have imagined, and created avenues for further contact and understanding. This made a real difference in defusing tensions and improving the capacity of the neighborhood to deal with any problems that might arise—including vandalism and loitering teenagers. Years later, this particular website is still active, with stories now spanning the whole city.

Several features of this modest project deserve to be highlighted. First of all, the issues were approached on a human level and directly impacted the everyday life of the area. Second, the approach was proactive: the problems addressed in this project were not defined in terms of unsafety and the need to tackle small-scale crimes, nor did they focus solely on troublemakers. Third, by concentrating on common human values and intense interaction with the people, existing community groups could be connected, strengthened, and harnessed for a common good.

From this project, we can learn that in this kind of open, complex, dynamic, and networked problem situation there probably are no direct, quick fixes, and that it is crucial to understand the underlying structures of the specific situation. By exploring these underlying structures, we will start to see solutions emerge. A problem situation like social housing will have been approached in all its complexity, without any assumptions, generalizations, or convenient simplifications by stakeholders. Engagement in these issues involves quite a bit of courage and determination: as was mentioned in case study 3, networked problem situations can often be so incredibly complicated that people just give up on them and turn away. Yet we will see that the very complexity, openness, and networked nature of modern problems also hold the key to progress in these situations: in the Amsterdam example, who would have expected a historic museum to be a partner in directly effecting such a deep social change? Later in this book, case studies will illustrate that the plight of retail in a postindustrial society and even the train conundrum can be tackled fruitfully through the creation of new frames.

The inability of conventional problem-solving to deal with the new open, complex, dynamic, and networked problems is reaching a crisis point. And these types of problems will not go away. On the contrary, we will have more of these problem situations to deal with in the future—they naturally arise today because we live in a nexus between technological revolutions and momentous social and cultural changes. We have an unprecedented need to extend our problem-solving repertoire so that it can address these issues. In the next chapter we will encounter some of the deliberate strategies that outstanding designers have developed for navigating this terrain—and then we will explore how these strategies can be harnessed by contemporary organizations.

2 PIONEERS

THE YOUNG DESIGNERS FOUNDATION

To explore how design-based practices can provide an alternative to conventional problem-solving and can drive innovation, we will now investigate projects carried out by two pioneering organizations that use design practices to develop radically different approaches to problems. Together they have more than thirty years of experience in this area.

The Young Designers foundation (YD/) was founded in Holland in 1990 as Young Designers and Industry. Initially, it did just what its name says: create projects that helped young designers and artists get valuable experience by working on projects for major industrial partners. Since the late 1990s, the emphasis of the organization has shifted, and YD/ has become a cultural institution that initiates and develops design projects within the context of cultural and societal change—under the banner "Design for Society." Three case studies will give a first idea of what they do and how they do it. In the last section of this chapter, we will begin to extract lessons that can be applied across a wide range of organizations.

CASE 5
Turning around a business:
On new approaches to service delivery

At the end of the 1990s, the Young Designers and Industry foundation was approached by one of the world's biggest international employment services companies. The company supplied temporary staff to client companies, but they were having trouble cementing their relationship with the temporary staff—a relationship that is absolutely crucial for such a service. Initially, the problem was framed as the need to design a promotional gift to help develop a better association and greater loyalty. Two artists, working together in the collective Orgacom (see orgacom.nl) were commissioned to come up with proposals. They quickly got to the heart of the matter: the employment services company did have a huge problem, and it was not one that could be solved by simply designing a giftwrapped pen-in-a-box. The whole culture of the employment services company was based around the need to attract client companies, and it was going out of its way to be taken seriously by them. It had adopted a very professional-looking corporate style: an abstract modernist logo, standoffish gray office spaces, and staff that was trained to efficiently handle all the forms and complexities of temporary staffing contracts. But in the economic climate of the time, there were more than enough client companies that needed temporary staff—what the employment services company actually needed to attract was young people to *be* that temporary staff. All the elaborate corporate fanfare that they had adopted was completely counterproductive in this regard. Instead of selecting people who come in begging for work, the company had to become more attractive and inviting to these workers in the range of eighteen to twenty-five years old. The artists came up with radical proposals to change the company's practices in this direction. These inspirations included temporary offices at festivals and other places where young people gather, staff retraining modules that included some hilariously confrontational role play, as well as a complete overhaul of procedures to make the company much more people-friendly. Nine simple line drawings expressed how the company could place itself differently in the world, outlining nine completely different kinds of "offices": a "home office," a "theater office," a "soap," a "club," a "bus stop," etc. (see figure 2.1). Rather than using elaborate designs, the artists designed brain teasers to trigger the discussions that would build a context for real change. The same message was driven home on a direct human level by the role-playing games. The project was presented in a video, showing clips of the discussions it sparked at the firm. The Young Designers subsequently presented this to the board of the company. They had effectively developed the problem in a direction where it could be solved in many new and interesting ways (Pappers et al. 1999).

Figure 2.1
Some of the design proposals made to spark debate at the employment services company (sketch proposals by Orgacom).

CASE 6
The integrated living of mentally handicapped people:
On the unintended consequences of social policy

This project was commissioned by the Dutch Ministry of Health, Wellbeing, and Sports, and the initial partners were a foundation for care of the handicapped, a medical infrastructure institute, a major project developer, a building corporation, and a new media think tank. Fourteen artists and designers from YD/ were involved. To sketch the context: traditionally, the government policy in Holland, as in many other countries, has been to house mentally handicapped people apart from society. They were cared for in mental institutions that were often beautifully positioned in wooded, secluded areas of the country. While society took pride in the quality of the care that was given to them, the mentally handicapped were also hidden away from the general public. Recently, this policy has

been reversed: the new conventional wisdom is to encourage mentally handicapped persons to live their life as "normally" as possible. This includes rehous-
ing them to live independently in towns and cities, with some support from a
network of caregivers. This new ideology has had huge and largely disastrous
consequences for the mentally handicapped themselves. When they entered the
world of "normal people," their physical isolation was ended, but not their mental isolation. Just moving mentally handicapped people from an institution into
an apartment does not assure their inclusion in society; they tend not to integrate into their neighborhood and really don't know how to deal with city life.
Their new neighbors generally ignore the mentally handicapped: in the frantic
rhythm of their busy lives, they do not have the time or patience to deal with
them. As a result, the mentally handicapped are stranded in their apartments and
are desperately lonely. The Integrated Living project was commissioned because
the issues facing these people are complex and require creative solutions that
potentially involve many stakeholders, spread throughout our modern urban
society. A space for change needs to be created. In the course of early discussions,
the initial question posed by the ministry was drastically redefined. The ministry
had inadvertently cast the problem in terms of the need to care for the mentally
disabled, while the artists and designers immediately approached the mentally
handicapped in terms of their abilities. This was a first breakthrough, because
thinking in terms of abilities opens up the whole problem arena to consider how
these mentally handicapped people can actually contribute to urban society (the
following quotations, from members of the partner organizations, are taken from
Suyling, Krabbendam, and Dorst 2005). First, from a Ministry employee:

> The designers were right not to accept the fact that mentally handicapped people
> live outside society. They understand that the mentally handicapped have their own
> ambitions.

The question to be answered then transforms from one about care into the
challenge of looking into different ways in which the contributions of the mentally handicapped can be given shape and facilitated. That investigation took
many, very different forms. Said an employee of a partner organization:

> Some mentally handicapped people are at home a lot, so they can make a positive
> contribution to the social surveillance in the community. The safety and security in
> the community also increases through the presence of nurses and [caregivers].

Some of the young designers engaged deeply and personally in the life of the
handicapped people to deepen their empathy and get a feel for where solutions
might lie. One designer commented:

[In my research] I faced some problems, since this group of mildly handicapped people has difficulties in verbal expression, and social interaction. They are often illiterate, so you cannot send them a questionnaire or have a conversation in the way you are used to. Even communication by telephone led to strange misunderstandings.

In a thoughtful essay that was written especially for a publication about the project, Miriam Slob remarked that her experience in dealing with handicapped people was rooted in her own experience of growing up in a small village. The kids in her year at the village school were very diverse, and they naturally included some mildly handicapped children, and so she learned to deal with them as a matter of course. Since moving to the big city, ostensibly a much more diverse population, she had retreated into her own limited circle of people and did not meet handicapped people anymore.

Other designers explored the roles of the institutions and caregivers. They experienced firsthand how hard it is for a willing and committed person to even get access to the mentally handicapped. In the course of the investigation, it became clear that the overprotective attitude of the care institutions and the caregivers constituted a major contribution to the isolation of the handicapped. Inadvertently, the responsibility of providing care had been extended to protecting the handicapped from their new environment, including issuing warning signs not to open the door to strangers. The caregivers hadn't come to grips with the fact that in this new living situation, they can't completely protect or control the lives of their patients anymore. And of course, dealing with the risks of normal city life is difficult, perhaps especially so for people working in a medical institution (where risk is dealt with in very specific ways). This insight alone uncovers many new possibilities for improving the integration of the handicapped (figure 2.2). Often, the issues gained depth and humanity (away from mechanistic or technocratic lingo) by being rephrased as personal questions:

[An employee of a partner organization:] Are you, as a non-handicapped person, integrated into your neighborhood?

[A designer:] The real questions relating to this project are: why do people want to meet each other? When do they become friends?

As often at the end of a YD/ project, there are promising perspectives that can be developed further—not as "the big solution" to "the big problem," but as departure points that together provide a fascinating map of possibilities. There are many issues and avenues that need further thought and discussion—the role of "care" and the way care is institutionalized in our modern society has

Figure 2.2
Spread from the YD/ project book (Suyling, Krabbendam, and Dorst 2005).

surfaced as a major theme, and so has the strange relationship between "care" and "control." The experience of being involved in this unconventional problem-solving exercise has had a profound impact on the project partners.

> [An employee of a partner organization:] During the process, relevant concepts, such as the issues of loneliness, fear, personal mobility, protection of the mentally handicapped, and the individualism of modern society were "refined." This enabled us to approach these issues in a different way.

It is exciting to realize that all the new frames (ways of seeing) that emerged from the complexity of this problem situation enable innovation across the very different partner organizations.

CASE 7
Street fashion and identity:
On growing up in public

More recently, the Young Designers foundation's practice has evolved from a project-based approach to creating environments for innovation. Projects such as the ones described above are a powerful inspiration and stimulus, but they need a structural follow-up when it comes to really shifting people's minds and working practices. They require a real context for transformation. One party that quickly embraced this new way of working was a social housing association in Amsterdam that owns large sections of the western part of the city, mainly middle-sized apartment buildings from the 1960s and 1970s. The population has changed from the original Dutch inhabitants to a diverse multicultural mix of families. There are reasons to worry about the future prospects for the large youth population, for many of these young people are comparatively undereducated and not well prepared to climb the first rungs on the social ladder. The street culture in the area is quite negative and at times destructive (literally, but also metaphorically), with small outbursts of unspoken frustration. Teenagers seeking to form their own identity within such an environment could easily slip into a downward spiral. This much we know—but what can we do? In collaboration with a local vocational training college, the Young Designers foundation set up a fashion studio in which forty teenagers spent a semester (after school hours) creating their own clothing collections, with the support of ten fashion designers. Some of the mothers happened to be excellent seamstresses, and were hired to form a production studio to make the garments. The kids were put firmly in control; the fashion designers were there only to support them through the process. This was quite an intense adventure for everyone, a positive and empowering experience in a neighborhood where those are not easy to find. All the hard work was rewarded with an inspired collection (under the name We Are Here) which eventually was proudly presented at a big fashion show before hundreds of guests (figure 2.3). More importantly, many of the youths had achieved a creative confidence and developed a real sense of responsibility through the project. All kinds of talents emerged—some were born project leaders. This fashion studio concept has been run several times now, and it has been successfully transported to other cities. Initiatives like this have the potential to turn a neighborhood around, by helping a new

Figure 2.3
Spread from the YD/ publication that accompanied the fashion project.

generation find pride in the creation of a positive identity. The fashion studio concept created a new platform for these teenagers to perform on, a much more even and exciting playing field than the neighborhood normally could provide. Thus the program sparked a significant, formative experience in their lives.

THE DESIGNING OUT CRIME CENTER

In Australia, the New South Wales government's Department of Justice, Police and Attorney General established a Designing Out Crime (DOC) research center together with the University of Technology, Sydney, inspired by the long-running Designing Against Crime Centre in London (Thorpe and Gamman 2011; Gamman et al. 2012). Its remit is to use design practices to revolutionize the way we achieve safety and security in society. In its first funding period, 2008 to 2013, the DOC center has delivered around 100 projects to 40 partner organizations. Central to the DOC approach is the pledge to—wherever possible—avoid the creation of "countermeasures" to crime, as these countermeasures create a climate of wariness and fear that destroys the social fabric of our public spaces and our society. First let's turn to three sample projects will help to demonstrate the Designing Out Crime center's approach to solving the open, complex, dynamic, and networked safety problems that our societies face.

CASE 8
The entertainment district:
On creating infrastructure for the city at night

Kings Cross, the entertainment district in the City of Sydney, has experienced continuous problems. With its bars and clubs and its slightly grubby nightlife (it has a history as a red-light district), this area attracts about 30,000 young people on a Friday or Saturday night (figure 2.4). All the activity is concentrated along a narrow 500-meter stretch of road where the big clubs and many bars are located. The problems that occur include drunkenness, fights, petty theft (pickpocketing), and minor drug-dealing. Late at night, the situation often gets out of hand, there is sporadic violence, and people get hurt—sometimes seriously. This crime problem seems deceptively simple: the common solution would be to invest in extra measures to counter the excesses and to punish the perpetrators. Over the years, the government has been trying to solve this problem by using these strong-arm tactics, mainly through increasing the police presence and installing CCTV cameras. Clubs have also been encouraged to hire their own security personnel. All this visible extra security has now made the entertainment district a pretty grim public environment, but although the number of arrests has increased, additional security measures don't seem to enhance public safety.

Designers from the Designing Out Crime center took on this project, quickly reframing the issues that were presented to them by the local council

Figure 2.4
Kings Cross at night (picture by DOC staff).

as law-and-order problems, and looking instead into how this area could be decriminalized. The designers reasoned that this approach could be a valid strategy because the people who get into trouble are overwhelmingly young people wanting to have a good time, not hardened criminals. The problems might arise from the fact that a crowd of 30,000 young people is coming to an area that has very little structure to it. The disorganization of the area and its attractions creates a whole host of truly complex problems for the many parties involved. Using a metaphor (a "frame") to help us understand the issue, one could compare this situation to a large music festival (30,000 people on a festival terrain)—the fact that it happens twice a week is neither here nor there. To take this analogy further: how would one go about organizing a music festival? A well-run music festival would provide many facilities that were not available at all in the entertainment district, but that could easily be designed there. For one thing, organizers of a music festival would make sure that people could arrive easily but also be able to leave again when they wanted. In this entertainment quarter, the peak time of young people coming into the area is about 1 a.m., but the last train leaves at 1:20 a.m. Getting a taxi later in the night takes about two hours, if the driver wants to pick up people there at all (taxis tend to avoid this neighborhood). So once people are in the entertainment quarter, they are basically crammed into a single road until the trains start running again at six in the morning. That is ultimately very boring and frustrating. Apart from the obvious improvement of providing more trains, the designers also proposed as a fallback position a system of temporary signage on the pavement, to help partygoers reach a different train station (a twenty-minute walking distance) that has buses running throughout the night.

Returning to the frame of a music festival, festival organizers would create chill-out spaces and offer continuous attractions to make sure that people will move around, so their experience does not completely depend on what takes place on a single large stage. As it happens, this entertainment district has a few big clubs that are the main attractions, but there is very little else to do. As a result, young people who have visited a club and go back out on the street might find that the queue for the next one is several hours long. If they decide not to join the queue, they are out in the street with nothing to do. The designers proposed that this problematic pattern of behavior can be minimized by providing a texting service or a smartphone app, so that people can find out how long the wait for the next club is before leaving the first one. In addition, some of the laneways around the central street could be prepared as rest areas, with water fountains and a relaxed "lounge" atmosphere away from the crowds. Another obvious thing one would provide for a music festival is enough public toilets. This particular entertainment quarter has only three, one of which is underused because it is located in a rather forbidding-looking police station. Consequently, there is a real problem with street urination (not surprising, if you calculate the amount of beer being drunk on a typical night). Of course, the designers proposed introducing a system of mobile toilet blocks.

Over the years, the clubs had hired more and more security personnel and bouncers as part of the conventional approach to solving the alcohol-related crime and antisocial behavior issues. The designers proposed a system of very visible young "guides" in bright T-shirts, who help people find their way through the area and who are also approachable when help is needed. This proposal makes perfect sense: research has shown that people do not approach officials for help unless these officials are approachable for other, low-threshold questions too. These bright and cheery Info people create a more caring social environment, a stark contrast to the huge private-security men in black who lurk, Death Eater–like, in every corner. In fact, the introduction of these security personnel has, paradoxically, been a major contribution to the grim atmosphere of the area.

CASE 9
Save us from the bollards:
On safety in a public space

Circular Quay, in the middle of Sydney, is a truly spectacular site. The beautiful views of the harbor are framed by the iconic Harbour Bridge on one side, and the Sydney Opera House at the other side. It is a picture-perfect destination for millions of visitors every year. Unfortunately, these very qualities also make Circular Quay a high-profile site, and as such an attractive target for a possible terrorist attack. The DOC designers were asked to come up with proposals for averting such an attack, or minimizing the damage if an attack occurred. Initial investigations showed that it would be important to limit car access to certain areas of the site. The police counterterrorism experts, very much aware of this need, were on the verge of proposing the placement of dozens of massive bollards to achieve this end. But they also realized that bollards would all but ruin the site and make life very difficult for locals and visitors alike. To get beyond the yes-or-no-bollards discussion, the DOC designers knew the problem needed to be widened to include many more complex issues and a whole network of stakeholders. And there was no shortage of problems with the area that could be addressed in concert with the counterterrorism question. Apart from the uniquely wonderful setting, the public spaces around Circular Quay were actually not that great—just some large open squares with nothing much to do. The DOC designers seized the opportunity, and proposed a complete redesign of the area that would make it fulfill its potential of being a window to Australia for the millions of visitors who come through every year. Installing artworks, appropriate seating, planting eucalypt trees from the different states, building a small informal open-air stage for street performers, if done to the proper specifications, would all help to prevent vehicle access and save us from the bollards (see figure 2.5). To minimize the effects of an attack, the designers also proposed reducing the crush of peak-hour crowds in the area. Thousands of city workers now take the train from Circular Quay railway station, which is centrally located above the ferry wharves. By repositioning the entrances and exits to that railway station away from the center to both sides of the site, these city workers wouldn't need to wrestle their way through the throng of tourists milling around in the central area. This considerably reduces the mass of people there at any one time, and thus reduces the likelihood and impact of an act of violence.

Figure 2.5
Design proposals for Circular Quay (DOC staff project sketch).

CASE 10
Retail theft made hard:
On crime prevention at its most invisible

Shoplifting is quite a common crime, costing consumers billions of dollars worldwide every year, as retailers have learned to budget in a 10 percent markup for what they euphemistically call "shrinkage." Conventional measures to reduce shoplifting include using mirrors and CCTV cameras, installing warning signs, and hiring additional security staff. Evidently, shop design can also play a major role in preventing this crime, but this is where retailers and their designers face a strange paradox: to sell, the goods need to be displayed in a beautiful and tempting manner and to be easily accessible to prospective customers. Most retailers will reject any design intervention that they suspect could lead to a drop in legitimate sales and would rather live with "shrinkage." Yet there is a societal cost to shoplifting that has to be taken into account: it is often an easy "first crime" for young people to attempt. If it isn't nipped in the bud, the habit of stealing can easily lead to other, more serious crimes. And from a moral standpoint, we just cannot let this stealing go unchecked.

DOC researchers and designers were challenged to create solutions that would not decrease the attractiveness of the merchandise (and, if possible, would increase it), while preventing it from being stolen. The DOC project focused on a number of goods that get stolen a lot—the list includes small expensive items like cosmetics, but also batteries, clothing, and cans of baby formula. The designers quickly realized that the biggest thefts occurred where a black-market network existed to sell goods easily and in large quantities. They decided to concentrate on these situations, and reframed the problem as one of preventing large quantities of these particular goods from being stolen. This focus shifts the problem away from complete prevention, which indeed is very hard to achieve without making life harder for legitimate customers. Many different solutions were devised for the broad range of products. In the case of baby formula, for instance, the designers came up with a dispensing mechanism that only allows you to take out one can at a time—preventing a thief from sweeping an armful into a bag. The wheels of the dispenser are filled with sand which makes a gentle but persistent sound, warning shop attendants to take a look when that sound is heard for a longer period of time. Similarly, for clothing, a hanger was developed that is clipped to the rail of the clothing

Figure 2.6
The original situation, and the proposed new retail shelf design (picture by DOC students—group Kim/Kulmar/Yuliana/Choi/Lysaught/An).

rack. It can easily be released by a customer (with one hand), but you need to take the clothes out one at a time. To prevent the theft of cosmetics, the shelf depth was reduced, and the front of the shelf was replaced by a tilted panel with product information and advertising. As soon as a customer reaches for the product, the panel and the product light up (figure 2.6), reminding those with a bad conscience that they have just activated a motion detector. In this case, the development of the problem away from countermeasures and delving into the complexities of the specific theft situations has led to multiple frames that spark a rich field of possible solutions (Dorst 2011).

LEARNING FROM THE PIONEERS

These case studies provide a first glimpse into a different, design-based approach to solving problems, which overcomes the classic syndromes that obstructed progress in the cases covered in chapter 1. A first batch of general lessons can be drawn to inform the application of such design-based practices across a wider range of application areas and organizations.

The Young Designers foundation is a platform for experimentation with new design practices, and as an experimental platform, it has gone through many radical changes itself, too. What have remained constant over the years are the emphasis on working with young designers and young artists, the drive to really push the envelope of what design can contribute to the world, and a strong educational agenda inspiring young designers to extend their abilities and the scope of their work through participation in these special projects. After all, these projects are a far cry from "normal" design practice, where one generally starts with a question and designs a solution. In contrast, the YD/ projects start with the signaling of an issue in society and seek interest from a group of initial stakeholders to partner in an open process (a "quest," a true exploration) around this issue, shaping the questions that should really be asked. Within this quest, creative freedom is combined with the need for subtle analysis and a keen sense of the relevance of the chosen path. This balance between radical openness and goal-directedness is safeguarded by a dialogical approach, where designers and partner organizations come together regularly in meetings to question the assumptions and challenge the conventional ways of working. The openness that is needed for radical exploration requires all participants to step out of their usual roles and defined authority. This is often challenging for the people from the partner organizations, as they are pushed beyond their normal professional role and possibly their comfort zone. But it is equally hard for the young artists and designers, who have to focus their analytical and creative abilities on the development of questions rather than solutions. These complex processes are guided by the YD/ staff, acting as a "producer" of the conceptual journey. With minimal interventions, they ensure the quest reaches a depth where new approaches to issues can be found. This is the art of the YD/ practice (see chapter 8). Experience has shown that once core questions can be articulated, possible solutions generally arise very quickly—and these are sure to be nonstandard outcomes, far beyond the reach of where conventional problem-solving would have led. Despite their openness and the radical creativity involved, these projects are not vague, irrational, or random. Rather, their originality arises from careful, in-depth exploration. The YD/ organization has learned that to be successful, it is crucial to make sure that the people from the partner organizations are intrinsically and personally motivated; only a strong internal drive will sustain their involvement in these complex, multistakeholder quests, in which the nature of the outcome will become clear quite late in the game. Over the last twenty years, many organizations have discovered the value of these inquiries, and the Young Designers foundation has become well established within the Dutch cultural landscape.

In comparison, the practices of the Designing Out Crime center are much more prestructured, time-restrained, and goal-directed. Yet the DOC projects also radically break away from conventional problem-solving practices in their own manner. The starting point is often different, in that many projects the DOC center has taken on are "old" problems, problems that the partner organizations have already been trying to deal with for a very long time, but that have proven impervious to their conventional problem-solving strategies. Prevalent problem-solving strategies in the area of safety and security are very much focused on the creation of countermeasures, through erecting defenses (putting up fences), introducing CCTV camera systems, and resorting to strong-arm tactics to force people's behavior away from unwanted (illegal or otherwise), unfortunate patterns. Efforts in crime prevention have led to a subfield within criminology, crime prevention through environmental design (CPTED), which sets design principles for public places to make them less amenable to criminal activity. These principles generally make sense, but as is often the case with conventional problem-solving, they suffer from the twin sins of oversimplification and overgeneralization. In its projects, the Designing Out Crime center is careful to avoid this mistake and to look very broadly at the problem and develop situated solutions. A key strategy in the Designing Out Crime center is to focus on designing to facilitate behavior that we want more of, instead of focusing on the negative. Intensifying the good use of public spaces will crowd out their misuse (see case 8, the entertainment district example, above).

While the practices of the Designing Out Crime center are much more structured and methodical than the approach of the Young Designers foundation, they embody many of the same principles. The key common thread through all the projects is that the complexity of the problem and context are embraced as the inspiration for revolutionary solutions. The six case studies in this chapter show the strength and possibilities that a designer's approach can bring to a wide variety of problems. We can also see that the initial questions formulated by the commissioning parties are a direct result of their earlier problem-solving attempts—and that these questions are almost always aimed at symptoms, rather than core problems. Reframing these questions is the key to achieving innovative solutions.

In concentrating on these two pioneering organizations, we are seeking to understand the deeper value that design can offer to many different types of organizations. Translating what can be learned from these pioneers into lessons that can be applied to others is not straightforward. That is the challenge we will tackle in later chapters. But first, we need to delve deeper into design, and the key question for chapter 3 is: *What, then, is the core of what design can bring?* To answer this question, we need to understand what design is, and also what it is not.

3   LESSONS FROM DESIGN

FOUR QUESTIONS ABOUT DESIGN

In this chapter, we will use four questions to guide us on a quick run-through of contemporary design practice. In answering these questions, we will encounter salient aspects of design, as they have been described and explained within design research. Then we will briefly dwell on the anatomy of design, creating an overview of design practices that helps position the particular practices we will focus on in the rest of the book. In the last section, we will draw five key lessons from these design practices. These lessons inform the frame creation approach that will be introduced in chapter 4. But first: the four questions.

WHAT IS DESIGN? MISUNDERSTANDING DESIGN
The reader will have noticed that in speaking about "design practice" in chapter 2 we moved far beyond the prevalent interpretation of "design" as merely the creation of beautiful things. The design professions have developed dramatically over the last twenty years, and design practices have matured into a real alternative to conventional problem-solving strategies. Unfortunately, the way design is presented in popular culture and in the media doesn't do justice to the new reality of contemporary design practice. The design professions themselves have not worked very hard to dispel the old, self-servingly romantic, mysterious, and heroic images of the designer. For the purposes of this book, we need to clear up a few common misconceptions before we can begin to describe what design really is.
   Design is not just about creating beauty
In many design professions, a pleasing visual aesthetic is important but is just one factor among many that need to be taken into account in the creation of

the design. In my own field of product design, designers are torn between the requirement to create a product that is technically viable and ergonomically sound and displays marketable value and the need to make it visually attractive. The idea that design should always be about the creation of something beautiful has deep historical roots: the very first professional "industrial designers" were needed because the first manufactured homewares produced during the industrial revolution were often overdecorated monstrosities (Heskett 1985). Until that time, before the advent of mass production, middle-class culture had been restrained in its tastes by the costs of craftsmanship. Ornaments were expensive, and thus were a status symbol owned by the few. But manufacturing suddenly made ornamentation very cheap, releasing a veritable flood of curls and patterns on every available surface. Manufacturers kept heaping it on, believing the more, the better. The 1853 world's fair in London (held in the spectacularly modern Crystal Palace) was the first venue that brought these fruits of industry together, and the result was shocking to the beholder. The criticism in the world press was appropriately scathing. The exhibition served as a wake-up call for the need of a new aesthetic for industrial products, and spawned the profession of industrial design. Despite all the years of evolution away from these early form-focused beginnings, the image of beautification still accompanies the popular notion of design. As Foucault (2002) has shown, although ideas might follow one another in quick succession, the underlying "discourse" in society changes only very gradually. He was talking about mental health, but he could have taken design as an example.

Design is not all about ideas

This is another great and intransigent myth, and to be honest, it is one that the design professions have been reluctant to dispel. The popular notion about design is that it works like this: client gives brief to designer, brilliant idea is born, client is happy, designer becomes rich and famous. This virtually never happens. Only novice designers who haven't yet developed the skill and amassed the experience to work in a much more deliberate way will have to rely on "the idea" to save them, resorting to the superficial scattergun approach of brainstorming to hopefully catch it (Lawson and Dorst 2009). Such a trial-and-error process is time-consuming, confusing, and hugely inefficient. When creativity techniques like brainstorming are used in a professional design context, it is always in a very specific manner, to explore solution possibilities within a constrained setting (see Sutton and Hargardon 1996; Sutton and Kelley 1997). Professional designers do not focus on the generation of "the idea":

they approach problems in a very strategic, deliberate, and thoughtful way. This approach involves a lot of hard work, where inspirational ideas are helpful but never yield a complete shortcut to a quality solution. Yet the myth of the wonderful, magical, "divine spark" idea that suddenly occurs to the brilliant mind of the incredibly gifted has been quite irresistible to designers, and many of them when interviewed will readily reinforce this image. Unfortunately, it is too good to be true.

Design is not irrational

There is nothing "soft" or vague about designing. Despite a deceptive playfulness in the conceptual phase of a design project, design ultimately needs to be rigorous in its approach if it is to deliver results for the real world. An essential part of the design process is making educated guesses when proposing solutions; yet these guesses will be tested later on in the project, if not by the designer then by the confrontation of the design with reality itself. The best designers are all very strong analytical thinkers with an original and playful bent of mind. Exercising judgment based on a clear analysis is an integral part of the design disposition (Lawson 1994). People sometimes see design as irrational because designing is not a completely objectifiable, closed form of rationality: design is inherently open-ended, as there is always more than one solution to a design problem. Design is not about creating "solutions" in the same sense that we create solutions to mathematical equations, as absolute truths in an abstract world. Designers create proposed solutions that can be judged on a sliding scale of better or worse relative to the needs of stakeholders. To ensure the relevance of their proposals, designers have developed elaborate phase models and work processes to deal with the inherent ambiguity in their practices, building in checks and balances wherever they can. To quote Nigel Cross, paraphrasing Hamlet: "Yes, they are quite mad—but there is method to their madness" (Cross 1996).

Design is not mysterious

We actually know a lot about design: the activities it consists of, the sequence in which these activities often take place, the abilities needed to be a good designer (Cross 1990, 2004), and the path of development of these abilities (Lawson and Dorst 2009). Systematic design research has been around since the early 1960s, and there is a flourishing design research community that has amassed a wealth of knowledge. There is much more to be discovered, and the design professions themselves are presenting a moving target for research by continuously reinventing themselves (Dorst 2008, 2013b). Yet there is now a core body of knowledge about design that is largely beyond contention. The reader should be assured that although this book will use design in unconventional ways and stretch it beyond the limits of the traditional design disciplines, we will be building on a solid knowledge base that has been amassed over all these years of design research. It is this strong foundation that gives us the self-confidence to build bridges to other disciplines that have become interested in design practices.

Not all design is good design

In pointing out the value of learning from "design practice," we do not mean to suggest that all design is good or that all designers are equally skilled in these design practices. As in any profession, there is also superficiality and mediocrity in design—and many designs that make up our human-made world are hard to defend, even inexcusably awful. What we will be focusing on here is the practice of a select group of top professionals in the field.

WHAT IS THE PLACE OF DESIGN IN THE GREATER SCHEME OF THINGS? DESIGN AS A FORM OF REASONING

The case studies in chapter 2 show the strength and possibilities that a designerly approach can bring to a wide variety of problems. As we've seen, it is very fruitful to look at problematic situations in a way that moves beyond conventional problem-solving approaches, and to consider these problem situations *as if* they were design problems. The designers and artists who were involved in the YD/ and DOC projects somehow regarded these very complex problems differently from the people who had tried to solve them before. But what, then, is the core reasoning pattern they apply when they design? Is it really that different from conventional problem-solving?

This is a fundamental question which cannot be answered by giving examples alone. We need a bit of logic to help us attain a much deeper understanding of the reasoning patterns behind design practice. We need to step back and suspend the "rich" descriptions of design that make the case studies such a good read, and take the question of design reasoning back to its very basics. Formal logic can provide us with a simple group of core concepts that describes the reasoning patterns behind design and other professions. This "poor" description of design helps us to understand whether design is different from other fields, and provides us with fundamental insight about the value of introducing design practices into other professional fields.

To penetrate to the core of design thinking, we look at the way fundamentally different kinds of reasoning are described in formal logic, in particular, the way Roozenburg and Eekels (1995) have taken the classic work of the pragmatist philosopher Peirce into design research. At the very simplest level, we can consider the world to exist of "elements," such as people and things, and connections between these elements, captured in a "pattern of relationships" that we can observe through the interactions of these elements, and the "outcome" of a process in which the elements have interacted. This is very abstract—but as an example, we can look at the original problem situation of a complex case study like Kings Cross and see all the *elements* in the situation (the police, the various groups of youngsters, the clubs, the physical characteristics of the public space) interact with each other in certain patterns that define stable relationships— patterns of interaction which in this case are leading to an unwanted *outcome*, the problems of drunkenness and violence. This three-way distinction between "elements," "patterns of relationships," and "outcomes" gives us enough conceptual tools to analyze the four basic reasoning patterns that humans use in problem-solving, and to show that design reasoning is really very different from the other three. We will analyze these ways of reasoning by simply comparing different "settings" of the knowns and unknowns in the basic equation,

| **WHAT**   +   **HOW**   leads to   **OUTCOME** |

(elements)   (pattern of relationships)   (observed phenomenon)

The four basic ways of reasoning that we will compare are deduction, induction, (normal) abduction, and design abduction.

Deduction—solid reasoning from cause to effect

At the start of a process of deduction, we know the "elements" in the situation, and we know "how" they will interact together. This knowledge allows us to reason toward an outcome. For instance, if we know that there are planets in the sky, and we are aware of the natural laws that govern their movement within the solar system, we can predict where a planet will be at a certain time. The calculations to support this prediction are very complicated, but in the end reasoning deductively toward a prediction is not problematic. With our knowledge of the elements in the situation and the pattern of their relationships (as defined by the laws of gravity), we know enough to safely deduce the outcome. Our forecast can be verified by observations, confirming that we have considered all the players in the situation correctly and have a sound grasp of the pattern of relationships through which the sun and the planets in the solar system interact. Of all the reasoning patterns we humans have at our disposal, deduction is the only one that is rock-solid. In terms of our simple equation, the starting position for deductive thinking looks like this:

Induction—discovering patterns
Matters begin to look slightly precarious in the next reasoning pattern, induction.

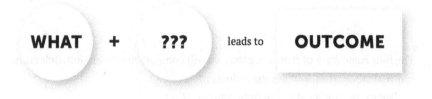

At the start of the reasoning process, we again know the "elements" in the situation, and—if we take the planets as an example—we know the outcome of their interactions in the sense that we can observe their movement across the night sky. But suppose we do not yet know the laws of gravity, the pattern of relationships that governs these movements. ... Can we use our observations of the movement of these planets to formulate such a law? We can't logically deduce such a law from observations. But we can observe the movement of the planets, and create meticulous descriptions. Those descriptions can inspire us to think deeply about the underlying patterns that could cause this behavior. The formulation of laws that explain this behavior is fundamentally a creative act, where the pattern of relationships is dreamt up and proposed.

Induction is crucial in the progress of science: astronomers propose different working mechanisms ("hypotheses") that could wholly or partially explain the observed phenomena, and test them by using the hypothesis to predict future outcomes, and check whether the hypothesis is true by matching it with observations. In the formulation of these predictions, we can again use the solid reasoning pattern of deduction: knowing the elements in a situation, and proposing a pattern of relationships between these elements, we can do our deductive calculations and predict where a planet will be in the future. Then we can wait until that moment arises, observe the planets again, and check whether the prediction was correct or not. If the planet is indeed where the hypothesis said it would be, we can cautiously say that the proposed pattern of relationships could be true. If the planets are not where the hypothesis projected them, the astronomer will have to come up with another possible theory of how these planets interact, and again use the power of deduction to test the new proposal. The progress of science comes from endless discussions between scientists who challenge and prove false each other's hypotheses until there is agreement that a certain proposed pattern of relationships is probably "true," because it matches current observations.

Detectives work in much the same way, or at least they do in novels: there is a group of "elements" (the suspects), and there is the undeniable fact of the dead body (the outcome of an unknown process). To find out what happened, the detective needs to create scenarios about how the murder might have happened, and scrutinize them through deduction (would this scenario of interactions have led to the murder, and the position of the body in the exact circumstances in which it was found?). This is pure induction, a creative act—even though Sherlock Holmes adamantly denies this creativity, claiming that it is all "deduction, my dear Watson." But by deduction alone, Sherlock Holmes would never have arrived at the scenario which exposes the murderer. Like detectives, scientists seem embarrassed being caught creatively guessing how something might work, and tend to claim authority by presenting their work as purely deductive (Kuhn 1962; Latour 1987). But it really isn't, and it fundamentally can't be.

Deduction and induction are the two forms of reasoning that we have at our disposal to predict and explain real-world phenomena, and they have driven our understanding of the world immensely. But deduction and induction are not enough if we want to *make* something. If we want to create valuable new "things," as in design and the other productive professions, the basic pattern of reasoning is called "abduction." In abduction, we set out to create a new "what"—a new "element" for the problem situation—so that the interactions in the system lead to a desired outcome. Abduction comes in two forms. In both forms, we already know at the beginning of the process something about the outcome of the equation; that is, we have an idea about the value we aim to achieve with the creation of the outcome.

Normal abduction—solid problem-solving, based on experience

In normal abduction, we know the result, the value we want to achieve through the desired outcome, and also the "how," a pattern of relationships that will help achieve the value we seek. The missing element is a "what" (an object, a service, a system), which still needs to be created. For example, faced with an undesirable situation of late-night violence in Kings Cross, we can choose to work within the established pattern of relationships for crime reduction, and send more police into the area in the early hours of the morning. Or we could—still within the same pattern—set up a training program for security personnel in which they learn to spot possible offenders more quickly. This is often what we do, create a solution within a fixed pattern of relationships. In this type of abduction, the degree of innovation will be limited because the problem-solving process doesn't question the "how," and therefore excludes the creation of new scenarios. Normal abduction is the reasoning pattern behind conventional problem-solving—using the tried and tested patterns of relationships to reach a solution. And this should not be dismissed: often the patterns of relationships that have been developed over many years of problem-solving efforts are more than adequate to deal with the problem situation at hand. But sometimes this type of routine reasoning doesn't lead to the desired value anymore, and we will have to think about the problem again. That brings us to the second type of productive reasoning, design abduction.

Design abduction—two unknowns lead to a process of creative exploration

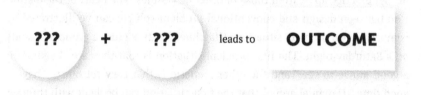

In design abduction, the starting point is that we *only* know something about the nature of the outcome, the desired value we want to achieve. So the challenge is to figure out "what" new elements to create, while there is no known or chosen "how," a "pattern of relationships" that we can trust to lead to the desired outcome. Thus we have to create or choose both a "how" and a "pattern of relationships." As these are quite dependent on one another, they should be developed in parallel. This double creative step requires designers to devise proposals for both the "what" and the "how," and test them in conjunction.

An example can help to clarify the difference between the two types of abduction: say that the *outcome* we want to achieve is an energy rush when coming to work in the morning. In normal abduction, we would also already know the "how," say that this is to be achieved through coffee—and we might even have a proposed method of brewing coffee (dripping, squeezing, using steam) so we can start developing a "what," engineering the machine to make the coffee for us. In design abduction, on the other hand, we would only know the goal (quick rush of energy before work) but not know how to achieve it. Hence, if we go for coffee, we would still need to choose a brewing method, create a design for a machine, and then judge whether this would do the trick

(Is it quick enough? Is it economical? Is it environmentally OK?). If none of the coffee machines we can think of will satisfy the criteria, we might need to start considering other ways of creating the energy rush.

To sum up: this comparison establishes the design professions as thinking fundamentally differently from fields that are predominantly based on analysis (deduction, induction) and problem-solving (normal abduction). But this distinction is not as clear-cut as it may seem from this logical analysis. In the real world, design practices involve a mix of different kinds of thinking—including inductive and deductive reasoning and normal abduction—that are the fundamental building blocks of conventional problem-solving. But there is a real fundamental difference, too—the nature of design abduction that sets the design practice apart from those of other disciplines. The heart of the distinction between design and conventional problem-solving can be illustrated by comparing two problem situations (Hatchuel 2002). Picture a group of friends on a Saturday night. The first problem situation is that they are "looking for a good movie to see," and the other scenario is that they set out to "have a good time." Hatchuel argues that the first situation can be dealt with through conventional problem-solving, but that the second requires design abduction. He lists three important differences between these situations. The first difference is that the design abduction situation includes the expansion of a key concept by which the situation was initially framed ("a good time"). This reasoning process requires a design process instead of a one-off choice of which movie to go to, from a limited set of alternatives (the movies that are playing that evening). There is no dominant design for what a "good time" would be, so imagination is needed to arrive at a definition. A second difference is that the design situation requires the design and use of "learning devices" to reach a solution. These "learning devices" include (thought) experiments and simulation techniques, in this case imagining different scenarios for going out. Third, designing the understanding and creation of social interactions is part of the design process itself. The group of friends needs to develop a way to imagine a solution, to share this view with one another, to judge the solution, and to decide which way to go (and experience shows that this process is not always easy). The process that these friends are going through undoubtedly includes stretches of conventional problem-solving, but it also contains these other "design" elements.

WHAT MAKES DESIGN HARD? PROBLEMS AND PARADOXES

Many issues that we encounter in our daily lives and professional practices never reach the status of "a problem." If the issue is quite simple and we have an obvious scenario in our repertoire to deal with it, we just get on with it and act. A "problem" occurs only when we either do not know how to progress or our chosen way of working gets us stuck. Then we have to stop and think, devise and critically consider options, perhaps be strategic and create multistep plans, do scenario planning, etc. Problems occur when something blocks our normal flow of how we deal with the issues in life. This "something," the counterforce, is bound to have its own background and rationale—at the core of really "hard" problems is a paradox. The word "paradox" is used here rather loosely, in the sense of a complex statement that consists of two or more conflicting statements (Dorst 2006). All the statements that make up the paradox are (possibly) true or valid in their own right, but they cannot be combined for logical or pragmatic reasons. There are three ways forward. The first option is to choose one side of the paradox and let it take precedence over the other. There is also the option of compromise, where negotiation might lead to a decision that sits near the halfway point between opposing needs and views. The third way forward in these tough paradoxical situations, where there is a real clash of views, standpoints, or requirements, is to redefine the problem situation. Designers do this very well. In her book *Ethics in Engineering Practice and Research*, Caroline Whitbeck (1998) remarks, "The initial assumption (within moral philosophy) that a conflict is irresolvable is misguided, because it defeats any attempt to do what design engineers often do so well, namely, to satisfy potentially conflicting considerations simultaneously" (56).

This observation is borne out by the case studies in chapter 2—somehow, the designers and young artists managed to wriggle out of confounding problem situations that had, in some cases, already existed for a very long time, and created a position from which the problem situation could be steered toward a solution. This accomplishment is in stark contrast to a conventional problem-solving approach, where the problematic situation cannot be redefined because the way the solution must work (the "how," its "pattern of relationships") is already fixed. This is the serious limitation of the normal abduction used in conventional problem-solving. The conventional problem solver only has the options of giving one side of the paradox precedence over the other or creating a compromise between the two positions.

The challenge of dealing creatively with paradoxes is one of the aspects that makes design so fascinating and captivating. Unresolved paradoxes can capture our attention to the extent that we cannot help thinking how to resolve them. Paradoxical problem situations inspire the creative imagination, much like the famous koans that are used in Japanese Zen training to provoke people to defy rationality and free their minds. While koans are beautiful and poetic, the challenge to come up with a sensible response can also be intolerable (Van de Wetering 1999). The mind-boggling nature of paradoxes and the difficulties they cause for our everyday thinking skills also make paradoxes a fascinating intellectual toy for linguists, logicians, and mathematicians (Hofstadter 1979). But that is not the way we want to talk about paradoxes in this book. Here we deal with real-world paradoxes that are caused by conflicting values and needs on the problem side, or by the incommensurability of design outcomes on the solution side.

In real-world situations, paradoxes are particularly formidable when the needs, interests, and "object worlds" (Bucciarelli 1994) are rationalized by different stakeholders. These perceived rationalities become a problem when a personal or institutional worldview is seen as the only one possible, making life hard for the problem solver, who is caught in the middle. Yet as Whitbeck has observed, designers can somehow deal with these knotty problems. In the Young Designers project on Integrated Living (case 5), the care organizations unquestioningly believed that part of their responsibility was to protect the mentally handicapped people in their charge. And they rationalized this "responsibility to protect" to include "complete control over their environment"—even if this meant isolating the mentally handicapped in their city residences. This result is, of course, completely at odds with the government objective of integrating these mentally handicapped into society. By being isolated, the mentally handicapped are further removed from companionship than ever (in the old days, they would at least have had each other to talk to) and are very far from being able to lead "normal" and "rich" lives in society. The paradox is complete. But one can see where some assumptions of the care organizations could be questioned, "cracked open," and investigated. Does "care" really mean "protect," and does "protection" really mean "control"? The government side of the paradox also needs to be unlocked: What are the assumptions that informed the ministry's thinking, in particular the presumed need to integrate mentally handicapped people in society? Are these assumptions valid? And what are the ministry's preconceptions about the role the care organizations would be playing in the new situation? Revealing the core paradoxes provides designers with an entry point for examining these assumptions.

HOW DO DESIGNERS APPROACH A PARADOX? ON FRAMING

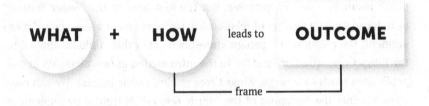

In questioning the established patterns of relationships in a problem situation, design abduction creates both a new way of looking at the problem situation and a new way of acting within it. This comprehensive new approach to the problem situation is called a "frame" within design literature (see Schön 1983, and appendix 2). Expressed in terms of the concepts in our logical formula, a frame is the proposal through which, by applying a particular pattern of relationships, we can create a desired outcome. If we go back to the earlier example, the problem of creating an energy rush at the start of the work day, then the choice of a chemical stimulus (caffeine) as a way to feel energized is the frame, the approach to the problem. But this problem might be reframed by proposing that there are also social ways of being energized (by an inspiring conversation), or by delving deeper and saying that what we really are looking for is not so much the energy rush, but a level of concentration—in which case, meditation would be a way to achieve the clarity of mind that is otherwise achieved by drinking coffee.

We call the act of proposing such a hypothetical pattern of relationships "framing." Framing is the key to design abduction. The most logical way to approach a paradoxical problem situation is to work backward, as it were: starting from the only "known" in the equation, the desired value, and then adopting or developing a frame that is new to the problem situation. This framing step is intellectually similar to induction: after all, we have seen that in inductive thinking a pattern of relationships is also proposed and tested. Once a credible, promising, or at least interesting frame is proposed, the designer can shift to normal abduction, designing the element that will allow the equation to be completed. Only complete equations with "elements," "pattern of relationships," and "desired outcomes" in place can be critically investigated, using the powers of observation and deduction to see if the "elements" and "frame" combined actually create the desired outcome.

In our Kings Cross example, strengthening the law enforcement approach didn't result in a desired outcome. But the metaphor of the "music festival" introduced a whole new set of relationship patterns (about access, crowd management, the creation of a benign atmosphere, etc.) that could be applied to the Kings Cross situation, and led to the introduction of new elements in this public area (such as signage, Kings Cross guides, public toilets). We can only learn whether the metaphor of the "music festival" is fruitful by implementing these new elements that flow from this frame, and observing whether the desired outcome of a more peaceable and less violence-prone nightlife in the area is achieved. Until it is thus tested, the proposed frame is just a possible way forward.

Earlier research into design practices (appendix 2) has shown that designers indeed spend a lot of time reasoning from desired outcomes via frames to possible design solutions, and go back again to reframing the problem when they suspect the design solution is inadequate. This reasoning pattern leads to the above-mentioned phenomenon of designers playing around with ideas, tossing up possibilities (proposals) for frames, relationships, and solutions in what may look like a childishly playful hit-and-miss process. Yet in doing so, design practitioners try out and think through many possibilities, building up an intuition about what frames might work in the problematic situation before they pursue one in greater depth. We have seen in the case studies of chapter 2 that designers naturally think beyond the current context (often much to the surprise of the other stakeholders, as in the "integrated living" case study). Designers realize that a real-life paradox is completely contradictory only in a certain, predefined *context*. Strategies to move forward from a paradoxical situation are based on the investigation of this context, exploring the assumptions that underlie the paradox.

This is a process of thinking around the paradox rather than confronting it head-on. The solution is not within the core paradox itself (which is stuck in closed definitions), but in the broad area of values and themes in the context surrounding the paradox. The richer this context, the more chance that fruitful avenues can be found to move forward. Thus, the very same properties of problem situations that are so challenging to conventional problem-solving—the open, complex, networked, and dynamic nature of contemporary problems that was mentioned in chapter 1—actually provide a rich field of opportunities for people with a designerly bent of mind. They need this richness to create a new approach from which solutions are possible.

In creating a frame, or a novel standpoint from which a problem can be solved, a design practitioner will say: let's suppose we use this particular pattern of relationships (in Kings Cross, the pattern was a "music festival") and see if we can achieve the outcomes we are aiming for. As Einstein once said, "A problem can never be solved from the context in which it arose." Apart from the obvious circularity of this statement (if the issue could be solved in its original context, it would probably never have registered as a problem), there is some wisdom here as the statement highlights the need for a problem solver to look at the context in which the problem was formulated. By looking at a broader context, the designers in these cases could frame the issues before them in a way that made the problem situation amenable to solution.

AN ANATOMY OF DESIGN PRACTICES

Design is a very broad field. In this book we are just looking for those elements of design practice that are potentially useful for dealing with open, complex, networked, and dynamic problem situations. Before selecting salient practices, we need a brief anatomy of design. Below, the core categories of design activities (figure 3.1) and the levels in design thinking (figure 3.2) are used to lay out the huge variety of design practices.

First of all, design practices are shaped around five general activities, starting with (1) the *formulation*, or identification, of the issues in a problem arena, which are then often framed in a new manner. (2) The *representation* of problems and solutions (in words, sketches, and sophisticated visualization techniques) allows the designer to develop his or her ideas in conversation with these representations. Designers tend to use multiple representations in parallel, where each representation highlights certain salient features of the solution that is under development. (3) The *moves*, or design steps taken, in manipulating the problem and creating solutions can be entirely original, part of the designer's repertoire, or in line with common design practices. (4) To keep a design project on track, there is an almost continuous *evaluation* going on. Early on in the project, this evaluation necessarily has an informal and

FORMULATING

UNDERSTANDING — IDENTIFYING — FRAMING

REPRESENTING

EXTERNALIZING — CONVERSING —
USING MULTIPLE REPRESENTATIONS

MOVING

CREATING PRIMARY GENERATORS —
KINDS OF MOVING — MOVING THE PROBLEM

EVALUATING

OBJECTIVE / SUBJECTIVE REFLECTING-IN-ACTION —
JUDGING ON 3 QUALITIES — SUSPENDING JUDGMENT

MANAGING

REFLECTING-ON-ACTION — BRIEFING —
PURSUING PARALLEL LINES

Figure 3.1
The spectrum of design activities (after Lawson and Dorst 2009).

subjective nature—later, the evaluations can be much more formal and objective. (5) Still, design projects are a challenge to *manage* because they are a mixture of a problem-solving process, creative freedom, and a learning process that is driven by reflection on action. Management challenges are exacerbated by the fact that the project brief is in continuous flux: as the possible design outcomes crystallize, the aims of the project can change.

NAIVE
RESULT-FOCUSED

NOVICE
CONVENTION-BASED

ADVANCED BEGINNER
SITUATION-BASED

COMPETENT
STRATEGY-BASED

EXPERT
EXPERIENCE-BASED

MASTER
DEVELOPING NEW SCHEMATA

VISIONARY
REDEFINING THE FIELD

Figure 3.2
The levels of design expertise and design thinking (after Lawson and Dorst 2009).

One can also consider seven general "levels" of design expertise (Lawson and Dorst 2009; based on Dreyfus 1992, 2002): (1) *Naïve* design is done by ordinary people in everyday life. It is often based on choosing from a set of design solutions or emulating (copying) an earlier design. (2) The *novice* explores what design is, and gets to know design as a series of activities that are organized in a formal process. The novice explores in order to discover the "rules of the game." (3) The *advanced beginner* recognizes that design problems are highly individual and situated. At this level, design problems are considered to be less amenable to the use of standard solutions than they were at the novice level. The acquisition of a language for discussing and criticizing design distinguishes this state of expertise from the previous ones. (4) A *competent* designer is one who can handle and understand all the common situations which occur within their design domain. Where the designer in the earlier stages of design-expertise development was essentially reacting to the problem situation, a competent designer actively steers the development of the design problem. As a result, the designer has much more control, allowing a design practice to develop depth over the course of several projects. (5) The *expert* is known for an approach or set of values that is expressed through his or her design work. This level of design practice is characterized by an implicit recognition of situations and a fluent, intuitive response. (6) *Master designers* have taken their practice to a level of innovation that questions the established way that the experts work, and pushes the boundaries of the field. Such work is published (through pamphlets, reflective papers, interviews, etc.) for others to study. (7) The work of a *visionary* is explicitly aimed at redefining his or her design field. Visionaries express their radical ideas in design concepts, exhibitions, and publications rather than in finished designs.

Most importantly, these seven levels of expertise represent seven different ways of design thinking: choice-based (naïve designer), convention-based (novice designer), situation-based (advanced beginner), strategy-based (competent designer), experience-based (the expert), developing new schemata (the master), and for some visionary individuals, redefining the field. Each of these seven levels of design practice comes with its own methods, its own critical skill set, and its own mode of reflection.

The broad spectrum of design practices can be visualized as a matrix in which the five categories of design activity are crossed with the levels of expertise (after all, the activities can each be approached in at least seven different ways). And such a matrix could be made for every design discipline, from architecture to product design, visual communication design, fashion, animation, and so on. Design is a huge and rich field full of professions that hold many different practices. Out of this vast repertoire of design practices, we will mainly focus on the "formulating" activity, as it has surfaced in the earlier analysis of reasoning patterns as being characteristic to design. To learn from the best that design practice has to offer, we will focus on the more advanced levels of design expertise—the expert and the master—in order to learn from them how we can more effectively deal with the open, complex, networked, and dynamic problem situations we find ourselves in today.

FIVE LESSONS FROM DESIGN

With this focus in mind, we can now move on to describe five key design practices. They are the five lessons from design practice that we must learn from if we want to deal with open, complex, dynamic, and networked problem situations. These five practices—(1) coevolution, (2) developing problem situations, (3) handling frames, (4) exploring themes, and (5) fostering a discourse—are the building blocks for the frame creation model that will be introduced in the next chapter.

1   COEVOLUTION

In expert design practice, research has shown that the design problem is not fixed before the search begins for a satisfactory solution concept. Expert design is more a matter of developing and refining both the formulation of a problem and ideas for a solution in concert, in a process called coevolution (Dorst and Cross 2001). Coevolution involves a constant iteration of analysis, synthesis, and evaluation passing back and forth between the two conceptual design "spaces"—the problem space and the solution space (Maher, Poon, and Boulanger 1996). In doing so, the designer is seeking to generate a matching problem-solution pair. Roughly speaking, what happens is that a chunk, or seed, of coherent information arises from the problem situation, and sparks the crystallization of a core solution idea (the "primary generator"). This core solution idea in turn changes the designer's view of the problem situation. Designers then redefine the problem, and check whether the new definition still suits the earlier solution idea. Unlike the popular perception, the creative event in design is not so much a creative leap from problem to solution: the great Idea, the light bulb moment. Rather, a creative event occurs when a bridge is built between the problem space and the solution space by the identification of a key concept. Empirical research confirms that expert design involves a period of exploration in which problem and solution spaces are unstable until (temporarily) fixed by an emergent bridge which identifies, or frames, a problem-solution pairing. Studies of expert and master designers suggest that this framing ability is crucial to high-level design. Ideas can be described as the moments when there is a sudden "click" between a view of the problem and a possible solution. Once problem and solution fit together nicely, the result takes on an unassailable quality: a structure emerges that is simple and coherent and that integrates all the demands that had occupied the initial, messy problem arena. This is a moment of complete design elation, to see the abandoned explorations, worries, and chaos of the past months, days, or weeks all disappear into a neat solution idea. To quote Wittgenstein, reflecting on his creative practice as a philosopher:

We are aiming at ... *complete* clarity. But this simply means that the philosophical problems should *completely* disappear. The real discovery is the one that makes me capable of stopping philosophy when I want to. (Wittgenstein 1963, PI 133; emphasis added)

2   DEVELOPING PROBLEM SITUATIONS

Design practice can be described validly as the coevolution of problem and solution: expert design practices have as much to do with reformulating the problem as with the generation of suitable solutions. As I remarked earlier, the "design thinking" movement, which focuses on the ability of designers to generate solutions, might be leading us astray. If we want to learn from expert designers, we need to follow their example and shift our attention to the study of problem-related knowledge, skills, and strategies. And the coevolution model, as presented above, is only the beginning. It is based on behavioral studies in a laboratory setting (Dorst 1997) where designers dealt with a simple design task (see appendix 1). This provided an impoverished view of design practice, as the situation and time constraints forced the designers to find new frames very close to the given problem situation. As we will see, more significant reframing of the problem happens during free-flowing design practice, where expert designers essentially develop the problem situation itself. The possibility of developing problem situations radically shifts the scope of design practices: until now, we have considered the desired outcome (desired functionality or value) to be unalterable in describing design abduction. But expert design practice shows that even the desired outcome can mutate with the adoption of a new frame, enabling designers much more freedom to step away from the initial paradox. Research on expert graphic designers has shown that they use a multitude of practices to develop problem situations, and shift the intended outcomes of the design project (Paton and Dorst 2011). The designer thus has to maneuver from a situation where he or she is seen in the role of a "techni-cian" (the client knows exactly what is needed, which the designer then carries out) to that of a "facilitator" (the client knows what is needed but not what is required to achieve it) or an "expert" (the client has a partially formed idea, and the designer must use his or her expertise to negotiate a workable formulation of the brief). For these graphic designers, the preferred mode of working is that of "collaborator," where the client and the designer mutually work on framing the project in terms of both problem and solution spaces.

From the interview data, we find that designers use abstraction, or an emphasis on the future context in which the design has to function, to sway clients from a problem-solving approach to one that allows for the negotia-tion of new frames (Hekkert and van Dijk 2011). These are effective ways of steering briefing conversations away from specific outcomes to an exploration of deeper situational values. Designers use metaphor, contextual engagement, and conjecture to "destructure" the problem situation along with their clients to allow reframing to occur. "Mood board" discussions constitute one method designers use to invoke metaphors and analogies. These mood boards assist in creating a more open conversation about a project, as they use abstract images that do not immediately prefigure particular solutions. The interviewed designers all cited contextual engagement through questioning and exploring the situation with the client as a key strategy. Reframing is further assisted by exploring abstracted, conjectured views of the situation. Often, multiple con-jectures are posed and are kept intentionally vague in playful conversations: "talking things through what we might explore." As the most significant barri-ers to reframing, designers cite the clients' fixation on their initial idea for the project, following a problem-solving mental model of design (where the client cannot imagine the designer taking a more strategic role), and resistance to journey (where the client feels the need for a quick solution and believes they lack the time or resources to open up the problem situation). In the field of product design, Hekkert and van Dijk (2011) have developed a formal approach to shift the definition of the problem by highlighting a future context. The first step of their model involves critically weighing the assumptions that lie behind the initial brief. To be able to create newness, the designer has to know the thought process that led to the design of current products and to the current problem situation. The designer then proceeds by questioning the importance of those fundamental variables and their current state. The next step is to cre-ate an image of the future context as it will develop. Once this has been agreed upon, the proper design process can begin, creating an outcome that will suit the future context. The client organization, which has been closely involved in envisioning the future context, will see the proposed design in light of this fresh context rather than the original one—this view makes it easier to accept quite radical designs. An example of such a project is the development of a "home office" desk for a mid-sized office furniture manufacturer. The initial brief was set with the normal constraints of a home office in mind: it is the smallest room in the house, it doubles as a storage or guest room, and you only go there when you really need to do some work. So a desk needs to be small, flexible in use, and have clever storage possibilities. Yet these are all assumptions, based on a very particular view of what work is (namely, the production of outcomes), and the role of work in people's lives (as a nine-to-five activity). In a society where "knowledge work" is becoming more important, and where people are encouraged to work at home to avoid the rush-hour commute to the office, the nature of "work" and the activities supported by a home office are changing fundamentally. Knowledge work is not only about production, but also about inspiration and reflection. Inspiration and reflection are not limited to normal working hours, and they tend to be highly connected and social activities. Thus, retreating to the small dusty "home office" room at the back of the house is probably not a good idea: inspiration and reflection need a much richer environment to thrive. After shifting the problem definition in this way, the designer developed an interactive kitchen table that takes center stage in the house. This table provides intense connectivity with the possibility of leaving digital documents lying about, in view for inspiration and reflection. They can be made to disappear quickly when the table is required for other purposes and be called back when a complete digital working environment when needed. Remember that the client was initially seeking a cheap desk design: shifting the view of what "work" will be in the future has created a new context for the product and opened up much more interesting possibilities. The interactive kitchen table, which would have been a crazy idea in the old context of seeing work as production, is quite logical within the new context.

Besides exploring the future context, the other major strategy that expert designers use to develop the problem situation is abstraction. This involves establishing a completely new context after abstracting from the current one, going back to the core values that must be attained. We will not dwell on this strategy here, as it is modeled and explained at length in the remaining chapters of this book. This peculiar type of abstraction is the core of the frame creation approach, and we will show how this design practice enables designers and others to deal with very open, complex, dynamic, and networked problem situations.

3   CREATING FRAMES

The slippery notion of a "frame" is central to the designer's ability to shift problem situations, and will naturally be taking center stage in this book. In this section we will investigate the nature of frames, and explore the ways in which designers deal with frames and the process of framing.

The first question should be, "What's in a frame?" Let's start with the example of Richard MacCormac's acclaimed chapel at Fitzwilliam College in Cambridge (Lawson and Dorst 2009). The original brief was to design a modern chapel to be built in one of the courtyards of Cambridge University. The flow of ideas led the team of very experienced architects in the direction of creating a round worship space that would look as if it were suspended in a square enclosure. This caused an acute set of problems for the design—how does one connect these very different forms? What is the nature of the relationship between these forms, and how can that be expressed through the detailing of the connection? After many fruitless hours of trying possible positions, formal solutions, and construction principles, one of the designers realized what they actually were creating could be seen as a "vessel" (a boat!). This key framing statement created a number of implications that the architects and construction engineers could fruitfully pursue. The relationship between a boat and its surroundings (the quayside) is, of course, one of a "mooring"—and it is easy to imagine which shapes would help articulate that "mooring" relationship between the suspended chapel and its enclosing building. The idea of a boat contains a very rich language of shapes (e.g., railings) and construction principles (e.g., beautifully curved wooden hull) that have been exploited in the final design. As this example shows, a frame is an organizational principle or a coherent set of statements that are useful to think with. Although frames can sometimes be paraphrased by a simple and elegant statement (as in the example above, using the metaphor of the boat), they are actually quite complex and subtle thought tools. Proposing a frame includes the use of certain concepts, which are assigned significance and meaning. These concepts are not neutral at all: they will steer explorations and the perceptions in the process of creation (Lakoff and Johnson 1980). Creating a frame is the result of a broader intentional action, which the frame then rearticulates with a new and interesting focus (Tzonis 1992). Frames should therefore be actionable—that is, they should be capable of leading to realistic solutions. For a frame to really come "alive," it also has to be inspiring and captivating. It should immediately draw forth mental images in the key people involved, and trigger solution ideas through a quick-fire stream of consciousness.

A frame is also a social entity, as it can help harmonize the thoughts of the various stakeholders within a problem situation. However, research has shown that this is not unproblematic: the communication of frames is not an easy matter, even among experienced professionals who have collaborated with the same team for years (Valkenburg and Dorst 1998; Valkenburg 2000). The problem is that frames are really only fruitful when they are fully embraced by all team members, and absorbed as an active thought process. For this reason, it's useless trying to communicate a frame by just blurting it out—if your team members are thinking about the issue from another perspective, they probably won't know what you are talking about. It is also not very productive to try to convince a team member that your frame is the right one: the frame is only going to be "right" if the team members find it inspiring and can use it to guide their own mental structuring of the situation. Thus, in the videotapes of designers at work used as data in Rianne Valkenburg's research project, when one of the designers tries to communicate a frame he just came up with, we can almost see him bite his tongue and resort to very long and quite abstract descriptive sentences. He thus suggests a frame by encouraging the others to arrive at the same frame idea themselves. Through these vague hints of a frame, the designer bypasses the adoption problem: people will usually adopt their own ideas much more eagerly, actively, and fully than those of others.

What is quality in a frame? While frames are content statements, and hence their quality in the end will depend on the specifics of the problem situation, they do possess generic qualities that are worth keeping in mind. Good frames ideally manage to create an image that spans and integrates a broad range of issues under consideration and might draw in even more issues from outside the original problem arena. Good frames are coherent, and provide a stable (noncontradictory) basis for further thought. Good frames are also robust, in the sense that the images they conjure up in the minds of the participants are sufficiently similar to provide a "common ground" for the discussion of the problem and possible solutions. Of course, good frames need to be inspiring and original—perhaps not completely new to the world, but at least new to the problem setting. And the best frames are very thought-provoking and lively, engaging people's imagination so their thoughts readily move along in the proposed direction.

Frames can often be episodic, in the sense that they are motifs that trigger ministories, opening up a whole world of shared experiences among people. With those common narratives comes the episodic, integrative knowledge that is needed to furnish a foundation for solution ideas. Many original design practitioners are great storytellers, capturing the elusive aspects of their frames by talking about their projects. All of these aspects of frames came to the fore in case 8, the entertainment district project. The key framing metaphor ("a music festival") contains a pattern of relationships that integrates new approaches to many of the most pressing problems that occur throughout the area, during all phases of a night on the town. The original statement transforms the discussion from one of criminality to one of the misdeeds of otherwise mostly innocent and fun-loving youth. The mental image of the music festival is coherent, in all its complexity, and it is robust in the sense that it can be easily understood and shared by stakeholders—many of whom will have experienced festivals firsthand, or have to think about them as concerned parents. There might be differences in interpretation or emotional response, but those can become the basis for a discussion that will only serve to enrich the imagery.

We must be careful and realize that "What's in a frame?" may not be the right question to ask—a frame is not a completely static concept. Frames are tools that exist within a world of actions and intentions, and whether some metaphor or pattern of relationships can be called a "frame" is completely defined by its use. "When is something a frame?" might be a better question to ask.

Once frames are accepted, they become the context for routine behavior: once accepted, the frame immediately begins to fade. Statements that started life as original frames become limiting rationalities in themselves, holding back new developments. Frames are best when they are "fresh." Creative and innovative people battle against fossilized frames, as we will see in the next chapters.

4 EXPLORING THEMES

Earlier in this chapter, a particular kind of abstraction was mentioned as the key strategy used by expert designers to develop problem situations beyond the core paradox. This is not "abstraction" only in the sense of going from the particular to a more general view of the problem situation: rather, expert designers move away from the problem situation toward the human dimension, seeking *meaning* in the realm of needs and values. This special design skill has evolved as a reaction to the fact that problem situations often arise when organizations try to tackle an issue through fossilized frames, in technocratic or bureaucratic ways. Judging from the case studies in chapter 1, the overly technocratic and/ or bureaucratic approach of conventional problem-solving in organizations is a significant part of our modern predicament. We have seen in the cases of chapter 2 that restoring the human dimension where it has been lost is an extraordinarily fruitful pursuit. In case study 6, understanding the nature of the loneliness that mentally handicapped people face when they are "reintegrated" into society leads to solutions that go far beyond the conventional framing of this problem situation in terms of care. The universal themes that drive the patterns of human behavior are manifold: they include the need to develop an identity, to feel at home, to deal with the loneliness that is an inseparable part of the human condition, etc. Arriving at these universal themes from the starting point of a concrete problem situation is not an easy process, and we will need much of the remaining chapters to explain the practices and strategies that expert designers have developed to traverse this difficult terrain. What the expert designers engage in is a subtle process of theme analysis that is very close to the practices used in "hermeneutic phenomenology" (van Manen 1990). But whereas in hermeneutic phenomenology, philosophers seek to reach a deep understanding of the human experience that underlies a text (hence "hermeneutics"), designers are interested in "reading" a problem situation.

Themes are a tool, a form of capturing the underlying phenomenon in a situation one tries to understand. Themes arise from the need or desire to comprehend—they are the sense we are able to make of a situation when we approach it openly, without prejudgment. The formulation of a theme is, at best, a simplification, helping us to distinguish a set of significant experiences and a deeper layer of meaning that underlies many observations. In hermeneutic phenomenology, distilling themes from a complex situation is described as a process of insightful invention, discovery, and disclosure. Philosophers have developed an extensive array of methods and helpful tools to systematically approach a text and to discover and formulate its themes. In his book *Researching Lived Experience*, van Manen (1990) for example describes the process of building an understanding of what it means for a child to be left alone by its parents. He systematically analyzes this theme by calling upon a broad array of sources: stream-of-consciousness texts, interviews, biographies, fairy tales, poetry (Milne), novels (Robinson, Blaman), films (*Sophie's Choice*), and philosophers (Buber) as sources for building up a description of the meaning of such an experience. (Nowadays he could also call upon the rich fields of cultural studies and sociology of everyday life: see Lefebvre 2008; Jacobsen 2009.) In his investigation of the theme, van Manen also inverts it and describes the lived experience of parenting as one of "a long goodbye." This theme captures the experience of the increasing distance between parent and child, the distance that inevitably grows as the child becomes more independent. This exact theme will be one of the lead sources of novelty in case 13, in the next chapter.

A rich ground for the deepening of themes can also be found in history. American historian Theodore Zeldin, for one, has written a history of ideas about many concepts that could arise as themes within frame creation projects (Zeldin 1994). For instance, in reflecting on an interview with a cleaning lady, he compares her feeling of dependence on her employers to the practice, in seventeenth-century Russia, of poor people selling themselves as slaves. The advantage they gained was that their new master was obliged to look after and feed them—in abdicating many rights, they freed themselves from responsibilities that were too hard to bear. His thoughtful exploration of the notion of (in)dependence creates an entirely new perspective on the interview and on the choices we all make in our lives. This example highlights an important feature of themes: themes always hang in the balance, they are neither good nor bad; and in the context of the problem situation, they do not belong to the problem or the solution. They just *are*. And they are universal, in the sense that they belong to the existential condition of all human beings. They are deeply personal on a concrete, human level and can be revealed through art— the theme of individual responsibility for life choices is exquisitely reflected in classic novels, such as the nineteenth-century *Oblomov* by Ivan Goncharov, as well as in contemporary novels, such as *American Psycho* by Bret Easton Ellis. Themes are truly timeless.

The systematic, deliberate, and multistep approach to theme analysis that the philosophers display is in stark contrast to design practice: although theme analysis is a crucial part of expert design practice, it is a largely informal process within design. Designers talk about "getting close" to the situation, they talk about the importance of "richness" in the problem area, and they stress the significance of getting "firsthand experience" of the problem situation to build "empathy." And yet they are quite vague about why they go to such lengths. Once they get into the problem situation, they seem to have no deliberate or systematic way of dealing with it. It looks as though they just hang around aimlessly. We would argue that they are observing clues that could lead to themes which will help them create a response to the problem situation. These clues are not explicitly expressed as themes, but are often packaged in episodic knowledge, as stories. For example, Hester van Eeghen, the internationally renowned bag designer based in Amsterdam, explained in an interview (Dorst 2002a) that she goes to the market on Saturdays just to observe people handling the wares they buy, and the various ways they hold their shopping bags as they grow heavier with every purchase. But her observations go far beyond these physical and functional aspects of carrying. She focuses on somebody, follows her around, and tries to figure out what kind of person she is (nervous? expansive?), imagining how she lives, filling in all kinds of details about her life. The value of design lies in the creation of a "something" for "somebody": creating this connection means shaping high-quality relationships, and Hester van Eeghen's spying on people is her way of getting a sense of what the basis for such a relationship could be. The bags she designs have a real cleverness and intimacy in the way they help shape this relationship, and as a result they are curiously satisfying to use. Some of her bags have an interesting trick that allows them to be worn in different ways, made with sensitivity to the user's real needs in different circumstances: what is a seemingly petite, elegant handbag can be expanded to hold A4 paperwork. A subtle bulge in one of her bags helps you bring an apple to work along with your laptop. Many of her bags have secret pockets that satisfy our deep-felt need for privacy. Just the knowledge that the pocket is there makes the bag more of a personal object, and creates a deep attachment (van Eeghen and Gannij 2009).

Likewise, famed Japanese product designer Naoto Fukasawa (art director of the Muji department stores) makes short video recordings on the street to observe how people use public spaces in Tokyo. A great example is the clip showing people on the platform of the metro, pacing while texting messages, and using the profiled stripes on the pavement that are put there for the orientation of blind people to guide themselves around the pillars. This brilliant observation tells you something not just about the use of these stripes, but about the state of mind of these commuters and how they navigate through public spaces. The understanding of people in this intimate way feeds into Fukasawa's very subtle designs (Fukasawa 2007).

Some designers go beyond observation and engage in deliberate interaction to unearth underlying themes in a situation. An example of such a strategy is the working method of the artists' collective Orgacom (see case study 5 and Dorst 2002b), which creates social artworks for organizations. Their strategy begins with immersing themselves in organizational culture. To shape their first understanding of the culture, they interview many people throughout the organization. Then Orgacom physically moves in and occupies a very visible location within the company (the restaurant is often a good spot) and, working in public, they create about ten proposals for artworks which represent different aspects of the organizational culture. The staff is encouraged to look over their shoulders and comment on the developing ideas. After about ten days of working as very public "artists in residence," they present proposals before the entire staff, who elect three or four for further development. Orgacom works on these proposals, developing a feasibility study and a price tag. The developed proposals are again presented to all staff and a final artwork is chosen. When the artwork is unveiled, Orgacom keenly observes the initial reactions to see how the work contributes to the discussion about the company culture. After all, this is a social artwork that needs to function in a social environment.

Please note that these curious design practices are analytical as well as creative. They are an intense form of sense-making, and include subjectivity and creativity in the act of giving precedence to some aspects of a complex reality over others. Themes are ambiguous in this respect—and this two-facedness is reflected in the ambiguous status that "themes" have within design reasoning: they are meaningful elements of the design situation, yet they are neither problem nor solution, but rather present a neutral ground that holds potential for development. They are on the cusp. All the projects that were described in chapter 2 have exhibited that moment of suspension, of ambiguity and tension—where the original problem has become almost insignificant and where all aspects of the entire problem situation are up in the air, so that they can come together in new ways. That is how new approaches were formed in response to problem situations as diverse as the entertainment district violence and the integrated living of mentally handicapped in society.

5 FOSTERING A DISCOURSE

Where do themes and frames come from, when they are not apparent in the original problem situation? In this section, we will look at expert designers' strategies when they create the physical and intellectual environment that nourishes inspiration and reflection. These multifaceted environments are the locus where the themes and frames that the designer stands for are born, articulated, and embodied, as well as explored, developed, and also discarded over time.

Within professional design practice, the "discourse" contains the practices and thought patterns that underlie the actions of a group of designers, say in a firm. This pattern is deliberate and human-made, and it is represented in the environment. When we study top design professionals carefully, we notice that leading designers take great care in developing their own discourse that underpins the manner of working in all the projects in the firm. As Ken Yeang reflects on the role he plays in his own architectural office:

> Any architect with a mind of his own, whether by design or default will produce an architecture which is identifiable to that architect. ... I had to study ecology, I had to study biology; that was the basis for most of my design work. I'm trying to develop a new form of architecture. We have this climatically responsive tropical skyscraper agenda and [in] each project we try to see whether we can push an idea a little bit further. ... I give every new member of staff the practice manual to read when they join. They can see not just past designs but study the principles upon which they are based. We work these out over time, over many projects. (quoted in Lawson and Dorst 2009)

The agenda of the firm is very clear, and there is a set of very deliberate activities and working methods which support that agenda:

> But in a project I have to be very dependent on my architects and each one of them has their own personal way of doing things, and I try to respect that so they are constantly improving and making things better, there is growth and they get motivated.

There is a very sophisticated way of creating a balance between continuity and change within the design practice:

> I do competitions more as an academic exercise. I treat competitions as research projects ... it motivates the office—gets them excited—lets the mind develop new thoughts and themes. I put all the drawings together and publish a book ... look in this book, these were our competition drawings for Kuala Lumpur and people said, "how can you spend so much time doing drawings and so on" and I say, "it's research, it develops ideas."

The projects and other activities, such as competitions, exhibitions, presentations, and publications, are seen as part of a very explicit strategy for developing the discourse into the future. Ken Yeang and other outstanding architects didn't report on directly interfering with the projects; apparently they influence what happens in their firms more subtly. They oversee the building and continuous development of the themes and repertoire of frames that together make up the discourse of the firm. This includes approaches to problems, strategies, particular knowledge, special skills, and a range of possible solutions that are all part of the common heritage. It contains strategic statements on the kinds of knowledge and abilities that must be brought together by the management to set the scene for projects, ensuring that they are in line with the company's "philosophy." The discourse is embodied in the physical spaces in which the designers are working (designers tend to "live" in their projects), the methods and tools they are expected to use, and the human resources policy. It captures the experience of the firm as it has developed (resulting in "common stories") for further use in upcoming challenges (Hargardon and Sutton 2000; Hirshberg 1998).

All together, the elements of the discourse, its frames and themes, constitute the intellectual capital of the firm (Coles 2012). The term "capital" can be taken quite literally here: expert designers are not approached by clients for the skills that they possess (these are often widespread) but for their approach to problem situations.

4   THE FRAME CREATION MODEL

FRAME CREATION

In this chapter, we will see how the five problem-focused design practices described in the previous chapter (coevolution, developing problem situations, creating frames, exploring themes, and fostering a discourse) can provide a new angle for approaching the open, complex, dynamic, and networked problems that were introduced in chapter 1. These design practices are well positioned to help us develop the problem situation, consider a broader context, build a deeper understanding of the underlying factors behind the problem, and most importantly to then create a new approach (or frame) to the problem situation. It is not hard to see how adopting these design practices could be useful in alleviating the syndromes that prevent organizations from moving forward. These lessons from design can, to some extent, be applied separately; for instance, some "design thinking" techniques that have been developed in companies and business schools utilize elements of "framing." But in chapter 2, we saw that the Young Designers foundation and the Designing Out Crime center have evolved a more comprehensive approach in which these design practices are combined to great effect. They have proven that the ability to create new frames leads to true novelty and innovation. My first encounter with this fascinating design practice through a project of the Young Designers foundation led to a twenty-year-long collaboration with them to explore its possibilities. In over 100 experimental projects, the frame creation process was honed in various problem contexts and on different scales of complexity, difficulty, and scope. These early insights sparked academic research into design thinking, including the study of problem-solving behavior in top industrial designers (appendix 1 and Dorst and Dijkhuis 1995) and multidisciplinary design teams (Cross, Christiaans, and Dorst 1996). This knowledge was diversified and deepened through the research of Rianne Valkenburg (2000), Remko van der Lugt (2001), Frido Smulders (2006), Christelle Harkema (2012), Bec Paton (2011), and others (see appendix 2 for the academic background story to the frame creation model). The Designing Out Crime initiatives in Sydney and Eindhoven then provided a real-world platform for rendering these research outcomes into a model, and for performing the first experiments toward the development of a methodology. All this knowledge and all of these experiences come together in the frame creation model (figure 4.1).

The nature of each of these nine steps will now be discussed briefly, followed by three case studies that will provide more details and a lively illustration of this fascinating new practice for achieving innovation.

ARCHAEOLOGY

The first step of the frame creation process is to investigate in depth the apparent problem, as well as earlier attempts to solve it. This analysis is crucial, as we need to delve deeply into the world of the problem owner in order to understand the past history of the problem. We investigate not only what happened but also what could have happened, what would have been different if they had chosen another path. If we didn't look at these alternative paths of action, we would run the risk of having our own perceptions caught in the same trap that led to the initial problem definition. This first step of "archaeology" also provides insight into the role the problem owner has had in creating the problem situation, and it gives a first impression of the dynamics of the organization over time. The analysis of the flux and potentiality of movement in the world of the problem owner should be balanced by an analysis of the hard, nonnegotiable boundaries ("They will never ..."). These nonnegotiable issues are important to know, as they will also limit the creation and adoption of new frames and solutions later on in the process. This broad-ranging archaeological analysis can be quite a lot of work, but seasoned professionals will quickly spot the strengths and pitfalls in the organizational setting of the problem.

PARADOX

Once the succession of actions that led to the problem situation has been defined and there is a clear understanding of what drives the organizational behavior of the problem owner, we move on to investigate the initial problem definition itself. The lead question is: What makes this problem hard to solve?

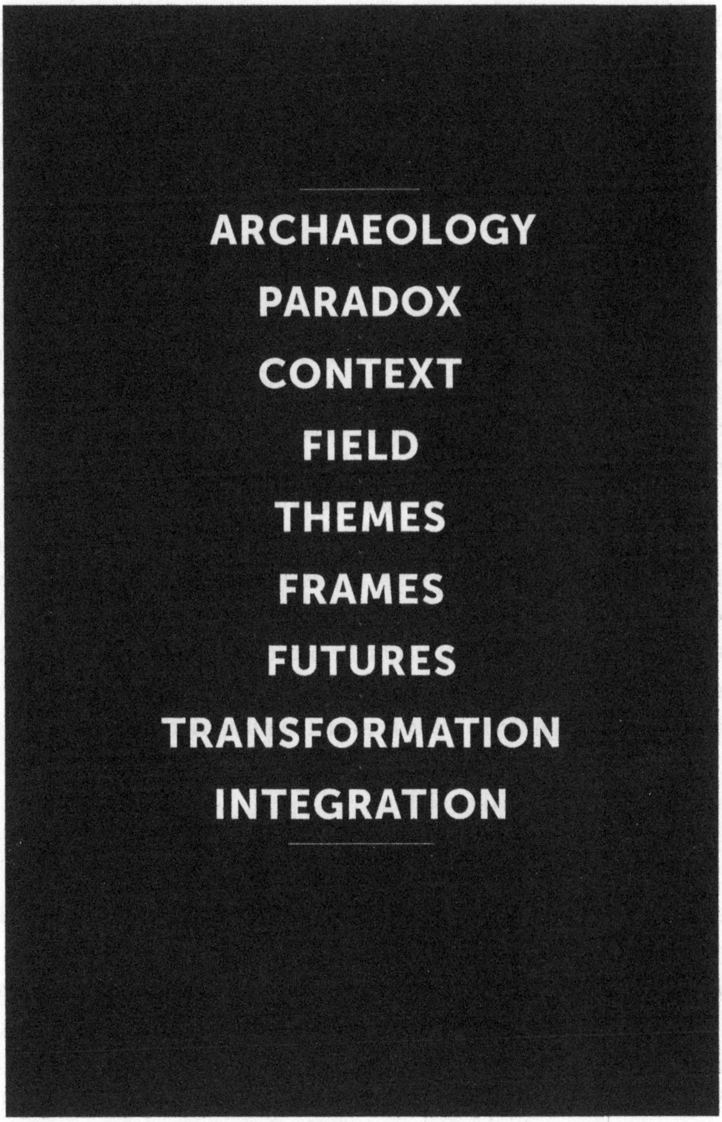

ARCHAEOLOGY
PARADOX
CONTEXT
FIELD
THEMES
FRAMES
FUTURES
TRANSFORMATION
INTEGRATION

Figure 4.1
The frame creation process model.

Often, several issues are intertwined in a problem situation, but to keep the frame creation process on track, it is important to take some time to identify the core paradox or deadlock that keeps the problem owner from moving forward. Within our experimental frame creation projects, it has proven practical to express the paradox as a clash of rationalities in a series of "because" statements. Please see the case studies below for examples.

CONTEXT

The next step in this analytical phase of the frame creation process completely surprised me when I first encountered it in the protocol studies of experienced designers: after all the hard work they do to establish and accurately formulate the core paradox, they put the paradox statement aside and do not look at it again until much later in the process. In retrospect, this makes sense: we need to deliberately turn away from the core paradox if we are to shift the problem situation. The designers shelve the original problem to begin the next step of the frame creation process with a sense of freshness and energy. What follows is an exploration of the practices of the inner circle of key stakeholders who have been involved in the problem situation before, or those who are clearly going to be necessary participants in any possible solution. By carefully examining them, we seek out significant influences on their behavior and what strategies they currently employ. In this way, we gain a sense of practices and scenarios that could become part of the solution.

FIELD

Once a reasonably complete overview is achieved (when there is saturation), we leave the inner circle of stakeholders alone and begin to radically widen the context, creating an intellectual, cultural, and social space we will here call a "field" after Bourdieu. Like many key concepts in Bourdieu's work, the concept of "field" can be approached from many different angles (Grenfell 2012) and requires some explanation. After all, we could take "field" as a meadow (not what we mean here), a "playing field" (close), or a "force field," as in science or science fiction (also really close). Bourdieu describes the notion of field as a space where assets (cultural, economic, social, and symbolic) are the "currency" that is exchanged between players. We will use the term "field" in this book in the sense of a very wide social and intellectual space. By creating a field, we consider all (potential) players, including anyone who might be connected to the problem or the solution at some point in time—actively or passively, just by exuding some influence. In mapping the field of players, we concentrate on their "currency," power, interests, values, and in particular the practices and frames they bring that could push the problem in a new direction. Importantly, our exploration of the field focuses on the deeper, universal values that will inform the formulation of themes in the next step of the frame creation process. By stepping back, we will see deeper patterns emerge, bringing to light areas where shared underlying values could lead to a new and promising direction. From this perspective, we often see new parties emerge as significant, leading to opportunities that have not been considered before.

THEMES

In theme analysis, we identify and seek to understand the deeper factors that underlie the needs, motivation, and experiences of the "players" in this wider field. A theme analysis ends with an understanding of the "universals," a selection of themes that are relevant to the problem situation on the deeper level at which players in the field have much in common. Because these universals are hidden beneath the surface of our everyday (professional) lives, it can be quite difficult to make them explicit. We are not used to discussing these deep themes in normal parlance. It takes exceptional circumstances for these profound human themes to be expressed (in eulogies, for example). But for the process of frame creation to work, the themes have to be very explicit. The elaborate methodologies that have been developed in hermeneutic phenomenology work through a process of filtering the texts or descriptions of experiences, finding patterns, and filtering these again until a core insight is achieved. The themes described in phenomenology are typically both deeply personal and universal. But themes are not strictly limited to these humanistic ones. For instance, designers of the Eindhoven Designing Out Crime center were delving deeply into traffic safety issues (see case 19) when the theme of "friction" began to emerge as a bridge between the human and the technical realm. This theme opened up a rich conceptual field, as "friction" can describe both a traffic flow blockage and the human feeling of being held back from what you want to achieve. Using the word "friction" also allows us to become more subtle in our thinking, realizing that blockages may be beneficial, even pleasurable (who would want to live in a frictionless world?). These concepts that bridge the human (cultural) domain and the technical or economical realms can be inordinately useful as themes.

FRAMES

Throughout the in-depth analysis of the broader field, common themes will emerge that can be different from those underlying the original paradox. Themes that are shared among many of the players in the field are particularly interesting, as they could be the basis for frames that are attractive to a network of partners. While these inklings can be a strong springboard, the ideation of a new frame is largely a creative leap. Again, experience with a varied repertoire of frames is clearly an advantage—having a team from diverse backgrounds can be inspiring for this step. As we have seen in chapter 3, the frame that results can be formulated as the implication that adopting a certain pattern of relationships (e.g., a metaphor) will lead to valuable outcomes. This implication can be written down as:

If the problem situation is approached *as if* it is ... , *then* ...

This may sound a bit convoluted, but it works—see the case studies in the second half of this chapter.

FUTURES

After a proposed frame is applied to the opened, broadened problem situation, it is then reshaped in a process of coevolution. Through these investigations, we are seeking assurance that the frame can potentially lead to realistic and viable solutions. This is a "thinking forward" exercise which is part of "design abduction" as it was described earlier (chapter 3). Only by proposing both a pattern of relationships and a design will we generate the feedback about whether we are on the right track in adopting a frame. It is important to remember that these design solution ideas are generated only for the purpose of exploration: they should be noted down but not pursued. Investing too much effort into any one idea at this stage might lead to attachment and a premature closing of the problem space while the quality of the frame that lies at the root of the idea is still being evaluated. In these playful explorations, we creatively envision how things might work. Experts tend to talk about this process of proposing and trying out frame ideas in terms of "fruitfulness": will a frame steer us in a promising direction, allowing us to generate multiple sensible solutions or not? Experts with years of experience will have built up an acute intuition about which frames will be fruitful and lead to results and which will not. Without this kind of experience and gut feeling, the exploration of future scenarios can be very time-consuming. In parallel with the development of these ideas, we also need to develop a fledgling version of the value proposition for all of the parties involved. A frame and the solution ideas it generates are only as good as the interest and commitment they spark in the parties who are needed to implement them.

TRANSFORMATION

The next step is a critical evaluation of what frames and solution directions would be feasible in the short term, or can be established gradually over a longer period of time. Here the representation of ideas becomes important as a means to explore their merit in conversations with parties in the field. This step is not meant to be a "hard" review of the idea as such, but rather an exploration to unearth changes that are needed in the proposed ideas as well as in the practices of the participating organizations, to make it all come together. At this point we also grudgingly have to weed out frames and ideas that may be great in themselves, but whose implementation would require huge changes in the practices of a stakeholder who has very little to gain. These frames need to go because they will never happen. This step results in a "business plan" accompanied by a transformation agenda and a strategy for achieving results. Often, because we are dealing with radically new approaches at this point, the strategy has a short-term component that will yield quick results (working with the organizations as they are now) and a long-term component that requires changing the practices of the various organizations (called "frame innovation"; see chapters 6 and 7).

INTEGRATION

In the last step of the frame creation process, we need to make sure that the new frames and the developments they initiate are well integrated into the broader context of the organizations involved (whether they are the original problem owner or a whole new network of players).The new frames created in the context of this original problem situation may also hold patterns of relationships that can be applied in other areas of the organization or beyond. New thinking means that new opportunities and connections will arise. On a deeper level, what has been learned in the discovery of the underlying themes can now be integrated into the "discourse" of the organization as active knowledge. This integration allows organizations to move away from only reacting to problem situations that the world throws at them, and to become proactive in their relationship to their environment. This is a crucial ability for organizations that face open, complex, dynamic, and networked problem situations.

CASE STUDIES

In the frame creation process, the oscillation between analysis and creation that is central to creative design practice is intimately combined with a movement of zooming in and out (from detail to abstraction and back again) and a shift in focus from an understanding of the core problem situation to widening the context, then to refocusing on the problem within a broadened field. Central to these movements is the fifth step, where a kind of design-phenomenological analysis leads to the basic themes from which new frames can be created. The first four steps lay the groundwork, and the last four steps explore the implications of the frames and the possible actions that they lead to. This description of the model above is quite abstract—let's see how this practice works in real life by applying it to three widely different problem situations.

CASE 11
The Sydney Opera House podium:
On inhabiting public space

The Designing Out Crime center in Sydney was asked to devise a new solution to prevent people from climbing up the "sails" (the white shells) of the Sydney Opera House. The initial two-hour frame creation session included a content specialist and eighteen young architects and designers from Sydney.

1 ARCHAEOLOGY OF THE PROBLEM SITUATION
The problem situation as presented to the Designing Out Crime center focused on the issue of people trespassing. Usually these trespassers would be protesters who climb the "sails" of the Sydney Opera House to unroll a banner or, in one case, paint a slogan on the sails of the building. These events have happened repeatedly over the years, and they always attract a lot of media attention. Thus, the Sydney Opera House, as an iconic building (a UNESCO world heritage site) and a highly symbolic locus for the city of Sydney, is politically vulnerable. Protesters have exploited key vulnerable locations at the bottom of the sails (which shall not be disclosed in this case study, for obvious reasons). However, it can be said that to climb the Opera House sails, a protester needs to access the podium on which the sails sit (figure 4.2).

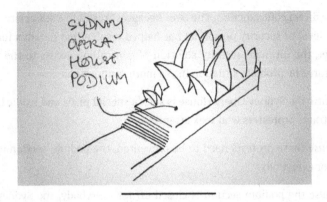

Figure 4.2
The Sydney Opera House podium.

The traditional security response to a problem like this would be to increase the level of security and to block or restrict access to the podium of the Opera House. Indeed, an eminent criminologist has suggested fencing off the whole area and charging an entry fee. An incident in 2005 confounded the traditional security response and the Opera House wanted a different solution—particularly because the podium area is a very beautiful spot to experience the special architecture of the Opera House, especially when the white sails reflect the light of the sun or moon. Over the years, many solutions have been considered, but it has proved difficult to reach consensus on what should be done.

2   ESTABLISHING THE CORE PARADOX

The core paradox that the Sydney Opera House originally faced, under pressure to take measures to prevent people from climbing up the sails, can be paraphrased as:

Because the Sydney Opera House is such a special place and an iconic building, it attracts protesters who seek attention.

Because the Sydney Opera House is such an iconic building, it cannot be touched/altered (due to heritage listing).

This is a direct contradiction. The two "becauses" result in a stalemate. Increasing the level of security personnel has helped resolve that paradox for a time. However, the ultimate security solution of controlling access to the podium would turn the problem situation into a more serious one:

Because the Sydney Opera House is such a special place and iconic building, it attracts protesters who seek attention.

Because these protests need to be prevented, the podium section is closed off for everybody.

Because the podium section is closed off for everybody, the Sydney Opera House cannot be fully experienced as a special place.

3   THE CONTEXT

The inner ring of stakeholders dealing with this problem situation include the Sydney Opera House as the "problem owner," as well as organizations such as Commonwealth Heritage, the food and beverage providers in the Opera House, New South Wales police, the New South Wales tourism board, the Sydney foreshore authority, the Opera House maintenance staff, and the counterterrorism police. These groups have all been involved in the various earlier attempts to solve the issue. The physical space for change is constrained by the "Utzon design principles"—a set of design principles and guidelines for modernization of the Opera House, provided by the original architect.

4   THE FIELD

The broader social field for the Opera House is huge: about 8 million people visit the building every year, mainly tourists from around the world. The field also includes the Aboriginal heritage of the site (the Bennelong headland on which the building stands is sacred to the Gadigal people of the Eora Nation), the patrons that go to the music concerts and opera performances, the numerous artists and performers themselves, art organizations, and other groups.

A major player in the field is the Opera House itself, as a physical reality as well as an "iconic" image that has become a symbol for Sydney and for Australia. Its design seeks to be universal, beyond any specific culture, and to symbolize freedom, youth, and hope. It is numbered among the wonders of the modern world. The podium space between the concert hall and the opera hall is the only place where one can feel surrounded by the building, as well as admire the wonderful detailing of the sails (the pattern of tiles), see the glow of the light, look at the sky, and enjoy the breathtaking view over Sydney Harbor. It is also quite an isolated space, a cul-de-sac with views that are framed by the architecture which can only be discovered by ascending to the top of the steps of the Opera House (most tourists tend to stay at the base).

5 THEMES

One theme that cannot be avoided is the conundrum of the Opera House as a cultural cliché: it is iconic as a photograph, but the millions of nearly identical pictures that are taken of the side view of the building from across Sydney Cove do not do justice to its intentions and complex reality. The steps up to the platform were meant as a spiritual, meaningful journey—to leave the city and everyday life and to enter a hallowed space where one can experience great art. This original aim, with its sense of intimacy and subtlety, is crushed completely by the sheer number of people around the building at any moment of the day. The deeper sense of being a special and significant place has gone, as well as (for most people) the building's connection to the arts. These values and intentions are overwhelmed by the strength of the building as a pure architectural sculpture. But that sculptural quality is largely visual and very static; the building has become a museum piece in its own right—the theme which emerges is that life needs to be restored to the Opera House on a subtle and human level, in line with its original aspiration. This could be achieved by exploring the notion of the podium space as a landscape in itself, where the elements of nature (wind, water, earth, and the sails as mountains on either side) come together in an abstract and impressive way. The abstraction and universalism of the architecture creates an ecstatic, uplifting, and rejuvenating feeling. The podium space also conveys a sense of refuge, an escape from the bustle of the city. This is the space where the spiritual intent of the Opera House can be most clearly experienced. The visitor experience could be one of the culmination of a journey, coming to a stop, and marveling about being there, in Australia, in Sydney. Engendering this sense of arrival on an existential level is another potential of the podium space. Yet at the same time, the Sydney Opera House is so well known that it is a member of a select group of international icons that are considered to be the universal heritage of humanity. Grouped with the Pyramids and Angkor Wat, the Opera House has become an international prepackaged must-see tourist attraction which does not connect to the city of Sydney at all. Earlier research has shown that the local population, known as Sydneysiders, avoids the headland where the Opera House sits. The interaction of Sydneysiders with the Opera House has become limited to concertgoers hurrying to the box office. While the Sydney Opera House is known among locals as "The House," it clearly is not a home to them.

6 FRAMES

Based on these three themes—"liveliness/rejuvenation," "spiritual uplift," and "the sense of place/home"—many frames were created and explored over the three-week period of the project. Some examples:

> *Example 1:*
> *If* the problem situation of the Opera House podium is approached *as if* it is a problem of providing liveliness and rejuvenation, *then* the podium should be ...

To bring life to what is a public space outside the city center, and make it function as a city square for Sydney residents, there should be a reason for them to come here, again and again—the space needs to be programmed to attract the desired segment of the population. Attracting local young people is especially important, as they bring a lively culture and could connect with the younger tourists (backpackers) visiting the site. They are also an underrepresented audience category for the Opera House. Attracting these young people could be accomplished through temporary exhibitions, pop-up events, light art, etc.

> *Example 2:*
> *If* the problem situation of the Opera House podium is approached *as if* it is a problem of providing contemplation or spiritual experience, *then* the podium should be ...

To bring stillness and a sense of peace to this outside space, one could work with the natural elements and subtly enhance the natural lighting to create spaces where the audience experiences a special effect—and make the experience of walking to the end of the podium (when you are drawn toward the view of the harbor) really different from the journey back toward the city. One could try to create a sense of dematerialized lightness, or weightlessness, in tune with Jørn Utzon's original sketches for the Opera House, in which the white sails have an open, cloudlike structure.

Example 3:
If the problem situation of the Opera House podium is approached *as if* it is a problem of creating a sense of place, *then* the podium should be ...

To convey a sense of place, of giving meaning to having arrived and being there, one could use storytelling to provide more depth to what the visitor sees. Accessing the rich history of this spot and the surrounding city and country could help. But then, a sense of arrival is also deeply personal—reflection and expression are both part of place-making. Perhaps there could be a way for people to leave a digital trace of their arrival, similar to carving initials in a tree.

7 FUTURES
By taking these frames as a starting point, and combining them where possible, one could envisage the mid-podium area as a twenty-four-hour curated space with diverse uses during the morning (perhaps yoga?), daytime (a sense of place created through a soundscape, storytelling, and/or providing background information), and late afternoon/evening (pop-up events, short concerts) to late evening (more meditative events, such as light art, or moonlight/star-gazing), combined with longer-term events like sculpture exhibitions, soundscapes based on the concerts inside the Opera House, interactive installations, and projections. Similar projections on the floor inside (in the foyer) and outside (on the podium) could be used to blur the boundary between inside and outside, visually creating the sense of lightness the architect envisaged in the original drawings (see figure 4.3). Thus the podium could be a fluid landscape, which locals return to all the time to drink in the new experiences. Alternatively (or additionally), one could guide the interaction of visitors by creating an elevated walkway that opens up interesting new vistas between the sails (similar to a treetop walk) while gently preventing people from touching the building and doing harm. In another scenario, sensors could be placed under the granite slabs that make up the floor of the podium, as part of the basic infrastructure to support all these different events. These sensors would be invisible and would not interfere with the heritage status of the building (figure 4.3).

To come back to the initial problem of the protesters: the around-the-clock use of the podium space would make it much harder for people to climb up without attracting attention, and some simple measures could be taken to slow down any attempted ascent so that security staff could arrive in time to prevent it. These measures only need to be in place in the early hours of the morning (when protesters tend to climb up, seeking to make the morning headlines) and to protect the highest of the sails, as this is the prime target. The infrastructure that is needed for the new curated use of the space could double as a security measure. The interactive floor could register if somebody is loitering suspiciously, or standing at one of the possible scaling spots for a very long time—and alert security before a climb is attempted.

8   TRANSFORMATION

While these ideas are attractive, and would certainly work to make the space more vibrant and create a safer environment through natural surveillance, their implementation would require a major transformation in the way the key stakeholders have been dealing with their "House." None of the present stakeholders on their own has the expertise needed to take on the complex curation of such a space, for so many different audiences, on an almost twenty-four-hour basis. The challenge for the Opera House organization will be to open up to the city itself, and allow other parties in Sydney to take turns in curating events. One could think of the excellent young artists' associations, a popular radio station, and the Museum of Contemporary Art, but also schools, youth organizations, universities, and other museums, as well as individual artists, designers, and the musicians who perform at the Opera House. The Sydney Opera House could organize competitions in which parties from Sydney (and further afield) could bid to host events and exhibitions on the podium. This idea ties in with the other aims of the Sydney Opera House (which include creating a better link to city, attracting young people, and of course increasing revenue), but on the flip side, it would mean that the organization must relinquish some control over what exactly happens, and fully welcome these temporary curators onto their hallowed grounds. As a result, they would have to deal with the same "care versus control" dilemma as the care institution for the mentally handicapped in case 6.

9   INTEGRATION

Once this program is under way, the idea of inviting the city to express itself on the podium opens up a myriad of possibilities. The Opera House podium could become an international attraction in its own right. On an intellectual level, this exercise is unique in giving new meaning to a static landmark that could otherwise become a hollow experience, and yet the concept is applicable to many public spaces worldwide.

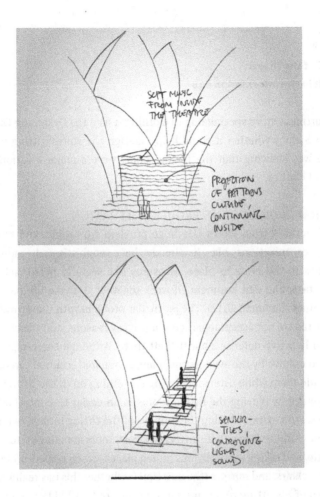

Figure 4.3
Possible future designs for the Sydney Opera House podium. (Sketch by DOC staff.)

CASE 12
Survival of the fittest:
On retail in the information age

X, a department store specializing in clothing, asked the Designing Out Crime center in Sydney whether it could help redesign the stores' fitting rooms, as evidence was showing that the fitting rooms were a major location for the stealing of clothes.

1   ARCHAEOLOGY OF THE PROBLEM SITUATION

Theft of clothing from stores is a huge problem worldwide, and highly professional organizations like X already have sophisticated, multifaceted approaches to the issue in place. Measures like security personnel, mirrors, cameras, tags, and exit scanners all work together to make life hard for the clothing thief (Gamman 2012). The particular problem with the fitting room is that cameras are not acceptable there for privacy reasons, and the clothes tags are the only active defense against theft there. Although these tags are very difficult to remove by the average customer, a prepared criminal can pull them off and hide them while ostensibly trying something on in the fitting room. X has responded by placing the fitting rooms in an easier-to-control area away from the store's exits, reducing the number of the fitting rooms, reducing the number of clothing items that prospective customers are allowed to take into the cubicle, and taking away obvious hiding places for the ripped-off tags, such as shelves, chairs, and mirrors (the question is whether this has really helped: a quick scan of X's fitting rooms produced dozens of tags hidden in double ceilings, wall partitions, etc.). Meanwhile, the size of the fitting rooms is also being reduced, as rising commercial rents put pressure on the stores to maximize the floor space for their stock.

2   ESTABLISHING THE CORE PARADOX

The initial design paradox here is clear: fitting rooms are meant to provide privacy, and thus they are good places for hiding criminal activity. These hiding places can also be misused to remove tags and hide them. There is no way out of this paradox ...

> *Because* the fitting rooms provide privacy to deliver a good shopping experience, they are good hiding places.

Because the fitting rooms are good hiding places, they become the location for theft.

Because the fitting rooms are a location for theft, measures are taken that reduce the comfort of customers.

Because measures are taken that reduce the comfort of the fitting rooms, they fail to provide a good shopping experience.

3   THE CONTEXT

The immediate professional stakeholders include the police, store designers, and the security firms that are tasked with reducing this type of crime. The big unheard party in the mix is, of course, the bona fide customer, who sees his or her fitting room experience being made miserable by cramped little gray cubicles where you can hardly move (let alone change clothes)—with nowhere to put your own clothes and bag (sometimes not even a hook to hang them on), and partitions that start rather high (to improve surveillance) and thus expose your own bag as you put it on the floor. The fitting room has become a generally unpleasant and grim environment.

4   THE FIELD

Clothing is a key expression of our identity, and as such it is a deeply social phenomenon. The greater field in which value is being created thus includes friends and family, as well as the broader social groups in society that potential customers belong to. The field also includes retail trends, as the retail market is going through major disruption to its business models at the end of the industrial economy (as discussed in case study 3). Retail is under pressure from online sales and urgently needs to find new ways of being attractive to customers. The initial kneejerk reaction of some store personnel is to chase away customers who they think are only coming to have a look at their products, but will probably buy online—needless to say, that strategy is not sustainable.

Because the Internet provides a good shopping experience, the brick-and-mortar shops are seeing falling sales.

Because the brick-and-mortar shops are seeing falling sales, they chase away potential customers out of fear they will buy the products online.

Because they chase away potential customers, they diminish the shopping experience.

In this case, the field actually yields a second, much larger question that should probably be taken up in the development project, as it will have an overriding influence on the design of the stores: the repositioning of the shopping experience in the face of increasing Internet sales.

> *Because* the Internet provides a good shopping experience, the brick-and-mortar shops are seeing falling sales.

> *Because* the brick-and-mortar shops are seeing falling sales, they need to understand the shopping experience.

This is not a paradox (yet), but an open question.

5   THEMES

The themes that can be identified in the field fall into two broad categories: those concentrating on the socially sensitive choice of an article of clothing in a private but isolated environment, and the theme of value creation in the live shopping experience.

6   FRAMES

The combination of these two paradoxes leads us to frame the problem as finding ways to support the social aspects of the choosing of clothing, and to bring this social aspect into the fitting room environment. This approach directly addresses the online sales problem: generally, the social sensitivity about shopping for clothes is well served by the Internet, which offers the possibility of sharing images and discussing items with friends before buying them. The main frame that the designers have worked on is one that will transfer this newfound strength of the Internet back to the store environment. This would mean turning the stores inside-out, as it were, to create an environment in which trying on clothes is the central (and unique and live) element that the store can offer. As a result, the proposal is not to hide the fitting room, but to make it central to the shopping experience and connect it to the broader social network of the shopper.

> *If* the problem situation of the department store's declining sales is approached *as if* it is a problem of creating a more fulfilling social shopping experience, *then* the fitting rooms should be … a catwalk.

7 FUTURES

As a preliminary physical design proposal, one could think of taking the idea of a catwalk to the middle of the store, with built-in cameras that allow the customer to post pictures online. The pictures could be put on social media where friends could vote on which of the alternatives should be bought. This concept can be extended in myriad ways—for example, a loyalty card could be swiped to gain access to the fitting room (thus making the fitting room less anonymous, but no less private), and the fact that you have identified yourself could be used to show whether the item you are considering would fit with the colors of the clothes you have bought on earlier visits to the store.

8 TRANSFORMATION

These ideas are not small or easy: implementation of such a reframed store concept would mean a complete rethinking of the logistics and supply chain of the company. Giving more space to the fitting room and communication would result in a reduction of the rack space, so the department store would have to reconsider displaying all clothes in all sizes on the racks (as they currently do). Stores would thus have to either reduce the clothing collection being offered or devise a new system. For example, customers might fit one item for size, then select the color and order the clothes through the store—either to be picked up later by the customer or delivered to the customer's home by the store. Yet these transformations are possible, and the pressure on the retail sector to reinvent itself in the face of growing online competition is strong enough to move it in this direction.

9 INTEGRATION

This frame sets the department store on the road to a whole new concept of quality in the retail experience—in a way, it is moving away from considering each client individually toward a more social concept of desirability and satisfaction. To get this right, the company will have to invest extensively in interaction with the particular groups it is targeting in order to build up valuable knowledge that can be extended into other fields. And finally, a sanity check: did the DOC designers, by radically broadening the problem field and taking on the extra agenda, actually help solve the original problem? The solutions as they have been developed to date certainly contribute to a less theft-prone environment: by taking the fitting room out of its hidden position, and

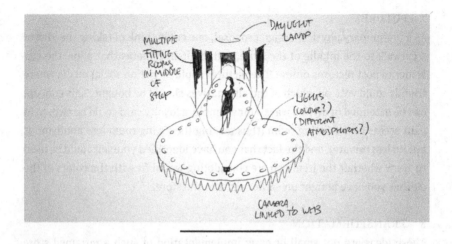

Figure 4.4
The "catwalk" as a proposed feature of a retail environment. (Sketch by DOC staff.)

catapulting it into the middle of the store, it becomes much easier to control and check. The additional idea of the card swipe for access removes the anonymity of the customer without reducing his or her privacy, and could be an important tool against repeat offenders (figure 4.4).

CASE 13

Daughters on the go:
On the perception of safety in the public domain

This frame creation session was carried out at Eindhoven University of Technology, as a response to a request by the Eindhoven city council. The information from several months of preparation was brought together in a two-hour frame creation workshop, with a content specialist and five experienced designers.

1 ARCHAEOLOGY OF THE PROBLEM SITUATION

In the center of Eindhoven lies Stratums Eind, an old narrow street with cafés and clubs that is a party spot for young people (particularly teenagers). The reputation of Stratums Eind is one of those urban myths: although the area was traditionally quite bad, the fact is that it has greatly improved in recent years through the joint effort of the city council, police, and club owners. But still, Stratums Eind is seen by parents as a risky destination for their kids. And because of its location, an evening out for these young people generally begins and ends with a lengthy bike ride from the suburbs to the city center. When looking at the police statistics, one can only conclude that going out to Stratums Eind is basically safe: nothing much happens. But the inevitable incidents are avidly picked up by the press, reinforcing the old reputation of Stratums Eind as a place of evil and danger. So the good parents of Eindhoven are worried—to be precise, it is mostly the fathers that are worried about their daughters (even though, statistically, boys are more often the target).

2 ESTABLISHING THE CORE PARADOX

Distilling the core paradox that makes this a difficult problem:

> *Because* girls like to go out, they bike into the city at night to party at Stratums Eind.

> *Because* they bike into the city at night to party at Stratums Eind, their parents are worried.

> *Because* parents are worried (and the media have picked up on this anxiety), the city has to respond.

The paradox arises because the intervening variable, the "the parents' anxiety," is largely a problem of perception. Clearly, improving the situation at Stratums Eind (which is what the media are clamoring for) is not going to be a solution. Nor would it be wise for the city council to merely communicate to the parents that everything is safe, and nothing will happen—this would expose them to criticism if something should happen to one of the girls.

3 THE CONTEXT

The context for this problem is that the city wants to be seen as fulfilling its responsibility, and the police want to be seen as capable and in control of the situation. But the press likes to sensationalize headlines, and the spectacular coverage makes parents deeply worried about their kids going out. Another player in the problem situation is the physical layout of Eindhoven. The city expanded rapidly in the 1950s and 1960s along a road infrastructure that is built for cars. Young families typically live in suburbs that are quite far removed from the city center. All of the city's through-roads are built for speed, with large sprawling intersections, and there are no houses directly adjacent to these thoroughfares. Although there is a good system of bike lanes and cycle paths along these roads, they tend to run quite close to parkland that surrounds the transport infrastructure.

4 THE FIELD

In the social field, we find the bar and club owners; they want to be seen in a good light, but do not want their business restricted in a way that reduces turn-over. This has been a difficult balancing act as the introduction of sweet high-alcohol drinks has made drinking alcohol more attractive to younger kids (the legal drinking age is eighteen). The public transport organizations (train and bus companies) see an interesting but problematic market: sudden peak usage is hard to cater for logistically, and they are wary of the drunkenness and van-dalism that can plague these night routes. The taxi companies are probably the only parties that profit from the status quo—they would like to see any solution include an increased use of their services. Most important are the teenagers and their process of growing up. They are exploring their own identities, oth-ers, and the world in an exhilarating but also difficult time in their lives. The key social groups in their lives are, of course, the schools they go to, as well as sports clubs and other organizations they might attend. The informal organiza-tion among teenagers is strong, as is their social sense and peer pressure—they are in the process of forming their identity by bouncing off those of their peers. As they become more independent of their parents, they can be fiercely critical of authority, and easily angered and emotional when approached in a way they see as patronizing.

5 THEMES

This problem arena is extraordinarily rich in themes. One major theme in the background is the question of how we deal with risk in society. Living is inevi-tably perilous, but in a society that emphasizes control, these dangers are not easily tolerated. People want the state to "eliminate" risk, though in reality risk can only be diminished. The second theme is responsibility: these teenagers will have to learn to manage the risk in their own lives. Their parents might be overly worried and protective, or they might be right in judging their kid to be too naïve to shoulder this responsibility. The parents are in the process of relinquishing control over their children (the growing distance between parent and child was one of the themes that Van Manen explicated; see chapter 3). Going out with friends without adult supervision is often one of the first major steps in this difficult process. This leaves parents worried, whether or not they have valid reasons to be anxious. A third theme at play here is that of the distance between the suburbs and the city—creating physical distance as well as emotional distance.

6 FRAMES

From these themes (dealing with risk, responsibility, and the distance between suburbs and city), many frames were generated. To name just two:

> *If* the problem situation of the clubbing daughters is approached *as if* it is a problem of failing to deal with responsibility, *then* the City of Eindhoven could ...

> *If* the problem situation of the clubbing daughters is approached *as if* it is a problem of (emotional) distance between the suburbs and city, *then* the City of Eindhoven could ...

7 FUTURES

One of the ideas developed on the basis of the first frame was the need for a key clip. The designer noticed that the girls going to nightclubs have no pockets to keep their house keys and the keys for their bike lock. Keys end up being stashed in bras or other tight-fitting clothing. He designed a clip that can safely hold the keys and can also send a signal to the parents to let them know that the keys are in place—thus subtly alerting them when their daughter is on her bike back home. The most important feature of the key clip is its different communication settings. The girl would discuss with her parents which one to use, thus demonstrably taking responsibility for her own safety. The introduction of these could be part of a school program to begin a discussion on the issues of safety and responsibility.

The second frame, distance, stirs up an equally rich domain of possible solutions. Although there are many ways to overcome the relative isolation of the suburbs, what makes this a difficult problem is that the parents live in the suburbs because they have chosen a certain lifestyle; they may even have moved there because it is a safe and healthy environment to bring up a family. When their children go out into the city, this splendid isolation is broken, the wall between the city and the suburbs is breached, and big-city problems begin to enter their homes. Yet now that their kids are growing up, these parents will have to learn to engage with the city to some degree. The City of Eindhoven can achieve this engagement by inviting parents to look around the Stratums Eind area as it is now, and explain all the safety measures that are being taken. The council should also introduce some solutions that actually reduce risks. For example, evidence shows that most accidents happen when kids cycle through a red light, and people on bikes are most vulnerable to other violence when they have stopped for a traffic light. To avoid these situations and ease the flow of bike traffic, the traffic lights along the routes from the suburbs to the city could be programmed in "green waves," visible through green and red LED lights on the side of the bike paths. While one is biking in the green zone, all traffic lights would be green. This measure also has the effect of causing people to cycle closer together, therefore increasing social safety. The city could also develop "bike stops" at Stratums Eind where kids who want to ride back to a specific suburb can gather and set off in groups (among friends, this could be supported by a smartphone app). The city could also take sophisticated measures to limit alcohol intake by encouraging other activities around Stratums Eind for which you need to be reasonably sober, such as urban sports. Event organizers use these clever tricks to manage crowds, and stimulating good behavior in this way really works.

8   TRANSFORMATION

At the core of these solutions is the need for the City of Eindhoven to influence the mindset of its citizens, in this case the parents of teenagers. As an organization, it is not used to doing so, except through single-issue publicity campaigns. But the themes of risk, responsibility, and emotional distance require a much more open strategy of dialogue and engagement. This goal could be accomplished by using the networks of schools and other organizations in the suburbs for both youth and parents, rallying them around the themes of risk and responsibility. Perhaps local media can play a crucial role by engaging the key stakeholders, who are most difficult to reach ... After all, it is only the girls themselves who can effectively allay the fears of their parents, and the city has to find subtle ways to support them in doing so.

9 INTEGRATION

Looking at the city through the filters of dealing with risk, responsibilities, and emotional distance is a fruitful exercise. Once these themes are articulated clearly, we immediately begin to see how the current fabric of the city supports or exacerbates issues in these areas—and immediately ideas spring to mind about how things could be done differently. On a completely different level, through this project the city might pick up valuable knowledge on teenagers' identity formation—an understanding that will come in handy when issues arise or a crisis occurs.

FIRST REMARKS

Five reflections follow on the nature of these case studies before we consider the frame creation model more deeply in the coming chapters.

First of all, we should pause to realize that while the design-based frame creation process may look self-evident when you read it here, it is quite revolutionary. It does not resemble a conventional, goal-directed problem-solving process at all—nor does it look like the innovation processes that have been proposed in organizational theory or innovation management. The key differences will be explored in chapters 5 and 6, respectively.

Second, we should realize that the results of these case studies do not resemble the kind of results that would have been achieved through conventional problem-solving. In conventional problem-solving, the Sydney Opera House podium would have ended up with a rather well-designed barrier to keep people out. The department store would probably have had a new system of tags and safety gates installed at the fitting rooms that would be harder for thieves to get around. And the City of Eindhoven would probably have launched another publicity campaign to point out the safety features of Stratums Eind. In fact, all of these solutions may still be part of the strategies that are sparked by the novel frames. But the reframing of the issues has both given a much better understanding of the real problem and pointed to a much broader repertoire of solution directions.

Third, the cases above are in fact snapshots of a crucial workshop that is part of a much longer process. As we will see in chapter 5 and more extensively in chapter 8, there is a process of project initiation and research that leads up to these two-hour frame creation sessions. The outcome of the session is a number of possibly useful frames that need to be explored in depth before a definitive choice can be made and the developers of the solution can be briefed.

Fourth: although these three case studies may give the impression that this process is extraordinarily elaborate and convoluted, the reader can rest assured that it feels quite natural, even when all nine steps are carried out in the short space of a two-hour workshop. The twists and turns in the reasoning patterns that characterize the different steps really build on each other fluently. One also may feel that this frame creation process takes the long way around to solve a problem where shortcuts would perhaps be possible. This is not the case. The frame creation model effectively and efficiently combines the five lessons we have drawn from problem-focused design practice in a simple, deliberate, and thorough process. The model's strength lies in the fact that the open, complex, dynamic, and networked nature of the problem situation is not denied but embraced: the very openness, complexity, dynamism, and networked nature of the problem is used as the road to creating a solution.

Fifth, and finally: the three cases presented here focus mostly on questions of the public domain, and thus gravitate toward the public sector. This tendency results from the fact that the public sector was the first to recognize the potential of the frame creation model. Now that the model is in place, leading commercial companies across a broad range of sectors are interested in taking the frame creation approach further within their respective domains, including healthcare, pharmaceutics, food, and transport. Early results show that the frame creation approach delivers equally interesting results in these domains.

5 THE PRINCIPLES AND PRACTICES OF FRAME CREATION

THE PRINCIPLES OF FRAME CREATION

The frame creation model as described in chapter 4 outlines a process, a series of nine steps that guide us through the complex practice of frame creation. The division of this practice into nine steps helps the problem solver by separating out different kinds of activities and sorting them into coherent units of thinking and doing, which can then each be evaluated as to the thoroughness and quality of their execution as the process moves on. A disadvantage of this process model is that it looks deceptively linear. While the nine steps of the frame creation model can be seen as a general and logical progression, in practice the activities that are captured in the steps all interact with each other—in a frame creation session there is a constant to-ing and fro-ing between the steps, and that is absolutely crucial in order to arrive at a good and balanced result to the frame creation process. The deceptively linear progression of the nine steps also obscures the fact that the starting point for a frame creation project can actually occur at any of the stages—the world doesn't always provide us with a neat "old" problem to react against, as was the case in the three projects presented in the last chapter. In the next paragraphs, we will see that new technical opportunities and entrepreneurial initiatives can also spark a frame creation process, as well as the pure inspiration that comes from exploring an interesting theme. In all these cases the starting point for frame creation is different and the process doesn't quite follow the progression of the nine steps.

So the nine-step model, while it is useful, should in no way become a straitjacket to the practitioner. To create some much-needed flexibility in frame creation, we will now move away from describing it in terms of a set process and describe the deeper principles of the frame creation approach to problem-solving. These deeper principles capture the core of this approach, and can be applied in processes of many shapes and sizes. For ease of use, the principles of frame creation have been expressed as ten "golden rules" (see figure 5.1).

The first four of these golden rules deal with the general principles that underlie the frame creation approach to problem-solving. The next three describe what "quality" is in the most important frame creation stages. The final three are strategies for applying frame creation in the broader context of organizational transformation.

1   ATTACK THE CONTEXT

The key principle of frame creation lies in its approach to a problem situation. Expert designers have shown us that open, complex, dynamic, and networked problems often cannot be solved directly, at least not in the terms in which they are presented. The problem and its formulation have their roots in a specific context that needs to be critically appraised and altered before the problem itself can be attacked. As we saw in case 6 on the independent living of the mentally handicapped, the problem as originally presented to the Young Designers foundation was described in terms of loneliness and isolation. The designers broke this mold in two consecutive steps: first, they realized that the "mentally handicapped" are a group that is defined by what they cannot do. Therefore, they are inadvertently seen as completely passive members of their new neighborhoods—a position that in itself contributes to their isolation. The designers escaped from this original frame of reference by looking at the possible ways these mentally handicapped people could contribute to local society, for example by creating appropriate jobs in the community. This would be a first step toward being recognized and valued, and to bring the mentally handicapped into contact with the people around them. In a second step, the designers realized that not only had the problem been framed in the wrong terms, but that a much deeper issue lurked underneath: because the organizations that care for the mentally handicapped felt they could only accept this responsibility by isolating the handicapped from their environment, they unwittingly contributed to the problem. It is important to realize that these deceptively simple insights can be achieved only by a thorough investigation of the problem context. If the designers had just taken on the problem in the terms in which it was presented (the mentally handicapped are lonely), their solutions probably would not have gone much beyond organizing occasional

ATTACK THE CONTEXT
SUSPEND JUDGMENT
EMBRACE COMPLEXITY
ZOOM OUT, EXPAND, AND CONCENTRATE
SEARCH FOR PATTERNS
DEEPEN THEMES
SHARPEN THE FRAMES
BE PREPARED
CREATE THE MOMENT
FOLLOW THROUGH

Figure 5.1
The ten principles of frame creation.

social events. Attacking the context allows us to move beyond the symptoms to root causes.

2 SUSPEND JUDGMENT

The frame creation process is aimed at opening new avenues and opportunities to get around an intractable situation. It circles the history and assumptions behind the rationalities that have led to the original problem formulation, as the problem-solving capacity of these rationalities has obviously been exhausted. While this is a critical process, it is certainly not intended to critique the stakeholders for lack of insight or to punish "bad" behavior. Within a frame creation process, the practices of the problem owner and the other stakeholders should just be taken as givens, which must be either worked with or worked around. To quote Aristotle: "thinking can start only once judgment is suspended." The deferral of judgment and preservation of ambiguity are precious qualities of the frame creation process (and they are surprisingly hard to hold off—we are so used to criticizing). Only in the last phases of the frame creation process is judgment necessary again, but then it is aimed at the newly created frames, solution directions, and value propositions. To pick up the example quoted above, one could feel frustrated with the caregivers' inability to grasp the difference between the patients' needs when living in a controlled environment like an institution and their needs in creating a new life in apartments in the city. While the fact that the caregivers did not understand their own role in creating this situation of heartbreaking loneliness is very relevant (as it is part of the problem situation, it will need to be dealt with), making judgments on their overprotectiveness will spark defensive or antagonistic responses that do not bring the solution closer in any way. Scapegoats are the last thing we need in frame creation. Actually, the fact that these caregivers think so strongly and implicitly in terms of control is an interesting observation in itself, worthy of deeper reflection. This notion that only complete control can lead to assured quality might be one of the key obstacles to be addressed in reforming the healthcare system in general, and possibly also other critical systems in our society. We will return to this idea later.

3 EMBRACE COMPLEXITY

Another key feature of the frame creation process is its drive to move beyond the simplifications that often underlie conventional problem-solving, and take on the complexity of the world as it is. This can feel quite counterintuitive: we tend to reduce the scope of the problems we face by introducing assumptions and framing them in a simple manner. Within frame creation, such assumptions that normally make life so easy are questioned, and the problem solver is invited to embrace the complexity of the situation. A major misunderstanding about the frame creation approach is that it contains some magic formula that makes problems easier to solve. On the contrary: one of its major features is that it avoids simplification. It only helps the proponent to deal with complexity by providing a distinction between diverse layers of context, which limits the number of elements and relationships that need to be kept in mind at any one time. But the frame creation approach initially makes problem situations much more complex, before we can allow ourselves to converge on a solution. Take for instance the Sydney Opera House case in the last chapter (case 11). In the course of the frame creation process, the Opera House organization was challenged to move away from seeing the issue as a security problem (difficult, but limited in scope) to engage with other parties in the city and cooperate to transform the role of the Opera House podium within the life of the city. In a sense, their problem has not been reduced—it has grown immensely. This principle of problem expansion, which is part of the frame creation process, could make the members of the "problem owner" organization acutely uncomfortable. But taking on this increased complexity is a crucial step toward creating new frames and solutions. If the scope of attention cannot be widened to a rich and complex field, no new frames can be created.

4   ZOOM OUT, EXPAND, AND CONCENTRATE

At the core of the frame creation process is a complex movement of zooming out and zooming in: first, widening the scope from a consideration of the problem itself and setting it in its immediate context, the problem owner. And then proceeding to the wider context, considering the other players that have been involved in the problem situation before. This first zooming-out step explores the players and the actions they have taken in and around the problem situation (and tries to understand which actions they might be prepared to take in the future). Beyond that, we expand our horizon to the broader field. This expansion toward the wider field is a rather special phase because we are jumping from the study of the behavior patterns of stakeholders into the realm of speculative thought, reflecting on what parties might be involved in the future and building up an image of how these parties understand their reality. This jump into the world of speculative thought then allows us to ponder the possibilities that are sparked by the emergence of common themes. From these "universals" we can create new frames for the problem situation, leading to proposed actions that can be critically appraised. Thus, the model of the nine steps might better be presented as two sets of nested circles, one of increasingly wider contexts of players and activities, and the other of thought patterns that increasingly converge toward action. These two sets of nested circles are connected at their widest point, by the emergence of meaningful themes that are neither problems nor solutions (see figure 5.2). And in the end, they are also connected at the most concrete level, where the solution born in this period of reflection should effectively address the original problem (thus linking the original paradox with the proposed agenda for transformation).

In case study 9, the problem of preventing a possible terrorist attack at Circular Quay was expanded to consider the open, underdeveloped nature of the adjacent squares. By physically enlarging the area under consideration, the designers came to consider a very broad group of possible stakeholders. For these partners in the field, the underdeveloped space is an opportunity to express the possible significance of this place: as a "showcase for Australia," the perfect destination point to welcome visitors and an opportunity to show what Australia has to offer. These ideas can then be translated into design briefs for objects to be placed in the public space.

5   SEARCH FOR PATTERNS

The beginning of a frame creation process can be seen as a deep and probing questioning of the initial problem situation. Yet this inquiry is a fact-finding exercise focusing on the "what," rather than a social or psychological inquest to try to understand the hidden depths of the problem. To ground the frame creation process, we can restrict the scope of inquiry to understanding the pattern of actions that people have performed, and the direct occasion that sparked their actions. Frame creation is a practice that is based on pattern recognition, and we need to pragmatically steer away from opinions or theories that people might hold about the world and about themselves. In the analysis and the creative steps of frame creation, it is the patterns of behavior that are key. It is the deeds that count, not the words. When we think back to case study 6, on the integration of mentally handicapped people in society, we can see why it is important to concentrate on facts and actions: the caregivers who create the problem by unwittingly isolating their charges are all wonderful, warm, and caring people acting with the best of intentions. It is hard not to be swayed

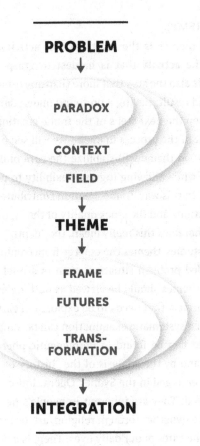

PROBLEM

PARADOX

CONTEXT

FIELD

THEME

FRAME

FUTURES

TRANS-
FORMATION

INTEGRATION

Figure 5.2
Frame creation as zooming out and concentrating.

by the way they deal with their patients, as we may mistakenly presume that the absolute integrity of their motivations will automatically lead them to the right actions. In this case, the problem lies exactly there, in the rift between "meaning well" and "doing well." The best example of this phenomenon is yet to come, in case 16.

6 DEEPEN THEMES

The creation of themes is the most abstract activity in the frame creation approach, and the activity that is hardest to grasp by people new to this approach. Yet it is also the step that more than any other defines the depth and quality of the end result. Having a profound understanding of the themes will not only help keep the next steps of the frame creation process on track, it is also a key benefit of the process in itself—we will see in the next chapters that a deeply understood theme will stabilize the core philosophy and identity of an organization, while allowing it great flexibility to cope with the fluidity of its environment. In this way, frame creation contributes to avoiding the chaos of knee-jerk reactions and the stuck quality of the "syndromes" that we saw in chapter 1. But what does this really mean, the "depth" of a theme? As we have seen in the case studies, themes can emerge from combining the riches gleaned from the expanded problem situation, even in a brief workshop session. But those particular themes should be viewed as nothing more than labels to indicate an area of interest that needs to be explored in earnest and at length after the session. Such a systematic examination can be supported by the extensive methodology that can be found in hermeneutic phenomenology, by design-based practices, and by the analysis of the "history of ideas" around a theme. The themes that emerged in the Sydney Opera House case study (case 11) are deep-seated indeed. They are inherent in people's need to aspire to a higher plane of existence (whether through religion, art, or the experience of nature), lifting us above the cares of our daily lives. There is a deep attraction to places that are out of the ordinary, that symbolize a higher significance, and where one can drink in that experience—albeit temporarily. The Sydney Opera House addresses these themes as a building. Understanding these essential meanings then informs the decisions that the management of the Sydney Opera House takes on the development of the site. Merely preserving the shape of the Opera House as a "museum piece" overlooks its real significance.

7 SHARPEN THE FRAMES

It is important to make the frames as sharp and precise as possible. A frame is only effective when it evokes a very clear picture in the mind, and when it does so for all the major stakeholders. Often, honing a frame to convey such a sharp picture can be achieved by combining themes or by combining several frame ideas. It often pays in frame creation to overdo this, and oversharpen the frames: for instance, in the case of the troubled entertainment district (case

8), one could (over) focus on creating a good late-night experience for just one particular group of youngsters (say, young males going out together—see chapter 8). Such very concrete and limited frames will more easily suggest what particular actions to take. The ideas that flow from such a focused frame can invariably be applied much more generally later on in the project.

8   BE PREPARED

What actually makes a "good" problem situation that would benefit from utilizing frame creation rather than using other problem-solving approaches? From the case studies, we can glean some general patterns: (1) there are opposing views or conflicting aims, (2) no obvious solution is apparent, (3) the problem can be placed in an expanded context, (4) there is an open-minded champion within the "problem owner" organization that is seeking a solution, and (5) earlier solution attempts have not resulted in a satisfactory resolution, to the point where there is a willingness to take a different approach. When most or all of these conditions have been fulfilled, the frame creation approach still requires a lengthy process of getting to know the problem, approaching actual and possible stakeholders, motivating them to participate, making contact with external expertise that may be useful, etc. Initial discussions with the problem owner usually involve "widening" the brief, often by involving not only the key decision makers but also the people "on the ground" in the organization who actually have a more direct and complete overview of the complex problem situation. This process cannot be rushed: together with the historic research that is an essential part of the archaeology of the problem situation, this pre-workshop phase takes on average two to three months from first contact. These activities can be seen as a "map-making" of the problem situation, in its current and in its expanded form. Experience has shown that these maps (see figure 5.3) are often a key deliverable of the frame creation approach, as they can act as mirrors helping organizations to understand why and how they are stuck in their problem-solving processes.

9   CREATE THE MOMENT

After all this preparatory work, the team can embark upon the frame creation workshop, which normally lasts two to four hours. In this workshop, all the information is brought together, and the team is taken through the frame creation steps by a facilitator. The team members of these frame creation sessions tend to be very diverse. To achieve breadth and depth in the frame creation

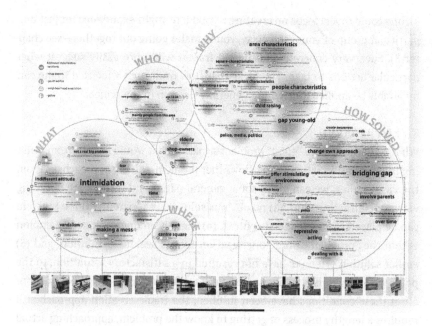

Figure 5.3
Example of a problem situation map (made by S. Duisters, student of the TU Eindhoven, for a project on "loitering teens").

process, participants are strategically chosen for the different skills, experiences, and approaches they can bring to the table. This is important because the frame creation process is a "creative analysis": while the process is thorough and always based on facts, the directions chosen are contingent upon the experience of the participants—different groups will take a different line of action. Included in such a team are content specialists who have a deep and broad knowledge of the problem arena and are able to feed fresh information into all the stages of the frame creation process as new questions come up. As in other design activities, the environment in which frame creation processes take place needs to be rich in inspiration and conducive to reflection (see chapter 3).

10 FOLLOW THROUGH

Frame creation doesn't end here: after the focused high-energy exchanges of the frame creation workshop, there is still much work to do. Experience has shown that it takes a couple of months to rework the session more thoroughly. One should check any assumptions that may have entered the discussion, dig into literature to achieve depth and thoughtfulness in the themes, sharpen the frames, make a much more exhaustive exploration of possible solutions and map these against the original problem, etc. The result of this follow-through is a report for the problem owner and key stakeholders, which is much more extensive and penetrating than the knowledge, insights, and ideas that are generated at the frame creation workshop session. After this report has been handed over, a lengthy phase of consultation often follows. As we have seen in chapter 3, accepting frames and adopting them as active principles to guide your actions is hard. After the adoption of one or more frames, the path to action can still be hard and long. New frames invariably disturb organizational cultures, processes, and structures that have been set up to support the conventional problem-solving approach of an organization. Moreover, in a networked world, these frames invariably cut through organizational boundaries in unexpected ways. It is crucial to support the problem owner in the hard task of following through on the path to action toward real-world, on-the-ground results.

FRAME CREATION PRACTICES

Until now, the frame creation process has been introduced in the context of a particular kind of problem. These problems are "old" in the sense that the problem owner and other key stakeholders have already done what they could over time to improve the problem situation. In these kind of situations, the archaeology step will dig up many earlier scenarios in which the problem owner and other stakeholders have already shown their hand. This step provides us with an intimate picture of existing frames and practices, as well as rendering a detailed view of what does *not* work in this problem situation. But, as discussed in the introduction to the chapter, we can encounter situations in which the problem is much more open than that, not so much a problem as an opportunity that could be addressed through frame creation. Or, alternatively, we can find ourselves confronted with a problem situation that is much more restricted, and provides no immediate way forward—where even an open problem-solving approach like frame creation has to take a step back and cautiously find a way to develop the problem situation before it can be fruitfully approached. Apart from these two extreme situations, a frame creation project can also arise from the inspiration that comes from the deep investigation of a theme. In this section, we will describe three projects to explore how the frame creation approach works in each of these cases. These case studies should be seen as exemplars of the different frame creation practices, from among the many that are possible.

First, we will describe a case in which a societal need and a new technical possibility require the creation of new frames. In this situation the frame creation approach can be used, though in a slightly different way: opportunity-based projects start more or less "in midair," as there is no set paradox or group of stakeholders. While this saves quite a bit of analysis work in the early stages of the frame creation process, the issues relating to the dynamics of the problem owner and the problem situation will then have to be assessed later in the frame creation process (in step 8, "transformation").

CASE 14
Smart Work Hubs:
On shaping infrastructure for the knowledge economy

All around the world, the nature of work is changing through the influx of new digital technologies. The coming of the digital age challenges the conventional view of work as the creation of outcomes in a central "production facility" that employees travel to. In a society where "knowledge work" is becoming more important, the nature of what professionals do is changing fundamentally. Knowledge work involves inspiration and reflection (Leadbeater 2001). These tend to be highly connected activities that thrive in a rich and lively (networked) environment. While the coming of the broadband network in Australia has encouraged people in small-town and rural areas to engage in knowledge work, the nature of these activities requires people to come together in new networks, which require a novel support infrastructure. The idea of creating "Smart Work Hubs" at major transport interchanges around major Australian cities are being piloted as the key physical infrastructure to match the broadband infrastructure. The framing challenge centers on the fact that there is no model for this yet: Smart Work Hubs in other countries tend to be generic work spaces where you basically rent a desk, rather than bespoke solutions that deal with the challenge of supporting knowledge work in remote areas. An initial frame creation workshop explored possibilities for creating a special Smart Work Hub infrastructure. A formidable group of stakeholders from various government departments used the frame creation process to frame the idea of a Smart Work Hub in a way that is intelligent, original, appropriate for the Australian situation (implementing a combination of government agendas), and also appropriate for the locations selected for prototyping—in particular, a site at the edge of Sydney's western suburbs.

1 ARCHAEOLOGY OF THE PROBLEM SITUATION

Because of the novelty of this challenge, the archaeology step in the frame creation model cannot focus on earlier solution attempts by the problem owner; instead, it can more neutrally investigate the initial situation of the project. In this case, the workshop focused on one proposed location, and began by mapping who currently lives or works there. Out of the very diverse picture, the image emerged of a suburban community where 70 percent of the workforce (mainly finance/media/communications/transport industries) commutes 1.5 hours into the city. There is also a small trade and manufacturing sector, aimed at local needs. It is a regional medical hub, and that cluster of activities is growing but lacks a research arm. Special to the situation are the highly educated people and creatives who travel through from the villages in the Blue Mountains (which form the western limits to the Sydney metropolitan area). As a regional center, it has only a small area of businesses and shops. The overall connectivity is good, by both road and train—which results in the center being quite empty during the day, when a whole population age bracket leaves for work and doesn't return until the evening.

2 ESTABLISHING THE CORE PARADOX

As the Smart Work Hubs are a novel idea rather than an existing problem situation, there is no paradox to investigate. Yet there are forces and developments to reckon with that could push a solution in opposing directions. These forces include the casualization of the workforce, the extensive decentralization of public services, and the delegation of functions from the public sector to the private sector. The creatives are an interesting group—but they have conflicting requirements depending on their orientation: locally operating firms need to collaborate closely in the delivery of their projects (in a "creative precinct"), whereas creatives with an international outlook have much wider-ranging needs.

3–4   THE CONTEXT AND FIELD

None of the possible stakeholders have been involved in prior solutions, so we move directly from considering these forces to the exploration of the broad field of players. For questions around teleworking, players include the management culture and the governance structure of major corporations in the city. We may also be dealing with regional centers that lie beyond the Blue Mountains. The strong agricultural sector in the area could be a major player that might profit from the creation of a new venue for information exchange, as it seeks to become more sophisticated and technology-savvy in the face of international competition. The statewide and national infrastructure parties (rail, road) need to be taken into account, as well as local government and local community initiatives—they could profit from the establishment of Smart Work Hubs. Existing major employers like the hospital and other specialist medical services could extend their activities. The finance industry could play an interesting role, as it is currently a leading proponent of teleworking, or working from home. And the needs of current and future inhabitants of the region would be the foundation for any new development.

5   THEMES

Three initial themes emerged from the workshop: (1) the sense of community as it plays out in a complex pattern across different scales; (2) the need for economic development that extends beyond the local level, and the challenge to support the collaboration and learning that will help achieve this ambition; and (3) the sense of work/life balance that comes from the community's location on the river, at the edge of the Blue Mountains National Park.

6   FRAMES

Because this was an initial scoping workshop in a very broad problem arena, the frame creation session led to a development process rather than the creation of specific frames. The themes provide the structure for such a process. The idea was to set the development process in motion by attracting a community of possible Smart Work Hub users to the area, support their learning through some prototype infrastructure (e.g., curated events), monitor the new

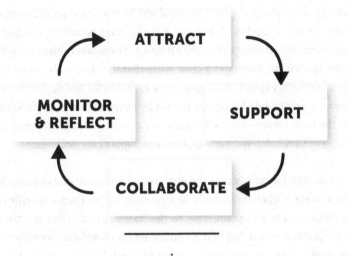

Figure 5.4
The Smart Work Hubs development cycle.

collaborations that emerge, evaluate the benefits (including personal benefits like work/life balance), and reflect on the kinds of infrastructure that would be needed to support these efforts on a more structural basis—while making sure that this infrastructure will be well anchored in the community (figure 5.4).

Frames can now be created for each of these steps—that is, a pattern of relationships and activities can be created to shape and support each step of the process. For the "attract" step, frame ideas emerged around the concept of a "health hub" that would include a research facility coupled with an education and work zone which would draw together students and professionals working in the same discipline. Students would be able to learn from exposure to a real-life working environment, and businesses would benefit from well-prepared local graduates. A frame idea for the "support" step was based on the development needs of the industries and services in the region: the Hub could be temporarily themed and curated to host learning and exchange on specific issues relevant to local industry (e.g., high-tech agricultural developments, new methods of water management, etc.). In the end, this process will help calibrate the framing of the physical hub that could still be patterned on different familiar models. Is this a market? A bazaar? A convention center? A precinct-in-a-building? A courtyard village? Or could it be a website, and remain virtual after all? In this discussion, there was a clear sense that the chosen metaphor should support strong and explicit place-making: a high-profile and desirable locality that makes it worthwhile for people to visit by providing easy access to the services of the local center—from child care, dry cleaning, and groceries to a gym, a selection of bars/cafés/restaurants, business support services, etc.

The key message for now is that the outcome of an opportunity-driven frame creation session is likely to initially be a process, rather than a specific frame. We will come back to this point later. At the opposite end of the spectrum, we encounter problem situations that are so incredibly closed and overdetermined that the problem owner really can't move forward. In these cases, the frame creation process can still be helpful, but now the starting point focuses on the "field" and "themes" steps of the process rather than looking at the archaeology. And the outcome of the frame creation exercise will again most likely be a process, rather than a definite frame and solution direction.

CASE 15
The weight of the world:
On identity and social housing

1 ARCHAEOLOGY OF THE PROBLEM SITUATION
The context for this project is an area in Sydney where the population tends to have low education level, low income, and a high unemployment rate. It displays a concentration of different kinds of disadvantage—people with problems in society gravitate here because, within a very expensive city, this is the very cheapest place to live. To visitors, the neighborhood looks closed, with lots of fences and walls. The few public spaces look shabby but nothing is really broken—they have just been abandoned. Nothing is spectacularly wrong, but there is an overwhelming atmosphere of boredom and despondency. The sense of helplessness comes from the realization that many people here have been overwhelmed by their various problems and forms of disadvantage; this culture focuses on day-to-day survival, and is passed on from generation to

generation as a new normality. Government and private initiatives (charities) have responded to the immediate needs of the area, but their many projects have been the proverbial drop in the ocean. In the face of such complexity, the Designing Out Crime center established a long-term partnership with the major social housing authority that holds local properties. DOC designers have been canvassing the neighborhood, talking to people to get a sense of problem situations that could be fruitfully addressed, and the solutions they envision.

The complexity of this situation defeats any attempt to come up with a single meaningful problem definition or paradox. The alternative is to ignore the plethora of problems, and aim the theme analysis toward building positive processes that will create a new core of solutions. When talking to inhabitants about what is important to them, we were surprised to find that the current dilapidated state of the built environment, which is highly symbolic to outsiders, was not an important problem to them. Low self-esteem and a lack of self-respect came up again and again as a root cause for their apparent inability to change the course of their lives.

5   THEMES AND FRAMES

From these conversations on meaning and value emerged the themes of identity (what is my essence?), aspiration (what can I hope to achieve?), and empowerment (how can I increase my self-worth?). But it is clear that single frames based on any one of these rich themes would still fall short of resolving the situation—they would have very little effect because there is not enough of a context; they need an overall structure in which the results of the projects could be taken forward. To create such a structured process, the designers realized that the themes needed to be combined, forming a "classic" transformation (learning) cycle if we add the activity of "reflection." This cycle then forms a meta-frame that delineates the steps of personal and societal transformation (see figure 5.5).

This transformation process became the central meta-frame for approaching the complex problem situation. As we will see, each of these steps needs to be framed and supported in completely different ways. To attain a clear and sharp frame that can lead to action, we need to concentrate our efforts on one section of the population that we see as being amenable to positive influence. The many young (teenage) mothers were singled out as an important group: it was clear from seeing them pick up their kids from school how much love and hope they invest in the next generation (the kids all looked immaculate,

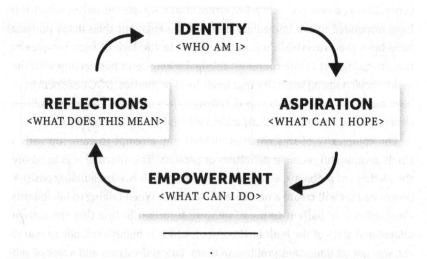

Figure 5.5
The steps of personal and societal transformation.

sometimes in stark contrast to their mothers). Wanting to do well for your kids is such a powerful shared value that it could be a forceful driver for change (bypassing the trap of low self-esteem). To establish a recognition and sense of pride for the identity of this group, a soap opera series could be developed to express their lifestyle and reflect it back to the people. To stimulate aspiration, the "local heroes" (people who have created a successful life but have often moved out of the area) should be persuaded to come back and help people see what they could accomplish and how. There might be small insights that could help lift the perspectives of these young women—if they could be persuaded to stay in the educational system just a couple more years before dropping out, that would mean all the difference. To empower these young women, facilities like childcare are absolutely crucial. As for reflection, just a couple of benches in the park where mothers can sit and talk when they pick up their kids from school could have an impact. A shallow play fountain for young kids would be incredibly beneficial, if it is designed so that the adults can sit on the rim and meet. You need social spaces so people can interact and value each other. There were many more frames and ideas built around other groups in the population—like restoring the natural flow of the streams and marshes (which are now ugly concrete storm drains) to make the area more attractive to outside visitors.

The strength of the frame creation approach in such a difficult area of interlocking problem patterns is that it undertakes a detailed exploration of the problem situation (by really listening to the problems of the people involved), and then takes a step back. The terms in which the issues are formulated are part of the problem situation, so the next step must be to explicitly create an alternative. In these serious cases, the solution doesn't lie in a single intervention but in the creation of a bigger process in which the themes work together. Transformation of complex situations requires this kind of subtle, concerted effort. In this way we can also assure that, as in all frame creation projects, the human side will lead to the development of the solutions—yes, in this case there are obvious things to improve in the built environment, but those improvements only make sense in the context of a deeper transformation process. All steps in the learning cycle of figure 5.5 are necessary for results to be achieved, and single projects that concentrate on only one or two of these steps are not going to have a lasting effect.

For the third of these cases to exemplify the variety of frame creation projects, we return to the Young Designers foundation, introducing a project that actually started from the investigation of a theme.

CASE 16
Loneliness:
On using frame creation for understanding societal issues

The YD/ project that was sparked by the crushing loneliness of the mentally handicapped people in an urban environment (case 6 in this book) has led to an interesting sequel, many years later. In this project, the theme of loneliness itself took center stage, as one of the contemporary problems that lead to unhappiness and suffering by many—and a problem that government bodies, health authorities, and NGOs are grappling with. The starting point for the YD/ project was that the use of the single word "loneliness" actually hides its many meanings. And the word is problematic, as it is tendentious, associated with shame—a real taboo that people do not like to talk about. There is a stigma associated with loneliness: you are a loser when you are lonely, which makes the feeling and the situation all the more painful.

5   THEME ANALYSIS

The YD/ artists and designers confronted this problem head-on by going out on the streets with sandwich boards, on which they had painted statements of their own deep personal questions about loneliness. This disarming approach led to many good conversations on the subject. A small documentary was made that showed how these people, interviewed at random on the street on a rainy day, were actually very thoughtful, open, and quite subtle in their approach to the issue. They saw loneliness as a normal part of human existence, and accepted it as such. Perhaps surprisingly, loneliness was even considered a situation that can be embraced and valued—a woman explained how the utter loneliness of a walk in nature had led to a change in her perception and a feeling of blissful connectedness. The idea that loneliness is a positive, that it can be a portal to reflection and insight, came up several times. Apparently there is more to loneliness than meets the eye. Together with a research institute and a philanthropic organization, the Young Designers foundation set out to explore this theme through artistic and designerly interventions. These interventions took place over a period of several years, and took many forms. Four examples: (1) an interaction designer created workshops in which people were drawn out to explicate the different types of loneliness they had experienced at various moments in their life. The trigger for this idea was the designer's use of the twenty-two Inuit adjectives for "snow" to create a typology of loneliness. By replacing the word "snow" with the word "loneliness" in these Inuit phrases, you get "gritty loneliness," "drifting loneliness," "melting loneliness," "light loneliness that is firm enough to walk on," etc.—beautifully poetic frames that really create an image of a type of loneliness that is possibly recognizable. These phrases helped people to get beyond the stigma that is associated with the notion of loneliness, and they were a rich basis for the subtle discussion in workshops. (2) In another intervention, an artist created an intricate form in which the interviewee is led through a series of questions on loneliness, through which people could both define their own experience in a sophisticated manner and wonder at the broad array of possible types of loneliness. (3) A photographer focused on a different side of loneliness as a lived experience. In her intervention, the "beauty of loneliness," the deep feeling of being utterly alone, is linked to a special sensitivity and quality of perception. She created a moving series of photos taken at such moments. (4) In a fourth intervention, the artist sits down to draw flowers with people. The drawing of flowers is an accessible, expressive activity that enables open conversation. Engagement with the idea of the flower is quite existential, as flowers are both an exuberant expression of life force and an expression of the temporary nature of life as they wilt and decay. Sitting side by side while drawing flowers allows the safe, indirect expression of the emotions that arise in the course of a deeply human conversation.

After the theme of loneliness was thus explored, the artists and designers came together and made a "nomological network" (see figure 8.3) to capture their experiences. This provided a rich overview of the real complex concept of loneliness, as a human and lived experience that comes in many guises. In the course of the investigation, the concept of loneliness gradually lost its purely negative connotation. In fact, the ability to "use and enjoy solitude" is one the eight factors that the U.K. charity the Mental Health Foundation lists as characterizing good mental health. Within Eastern spiritual traditions, this is called "aloneness," and the ability to be alone and in harmony is seen as a great achievement.

6   FRAMES

The subtle reflection of the artists' interventions has changed the direction of the project completely, away from seeing loneliness as a problem that should somehow be "solved" through an intervention. One of the most fruitful frames of those adopted for the second half of the project was that of "aloneness," or to put it in a more activist language: to be "for loneliness." This leads to thinking about loneliness in terms of the inner strength of people, and to thinking about possible ways in which people can gather and muster that strength.

7   FUTURES

This frame was applied to the plight of one of the groups known to suffer because of the loneliness of the position they find themselves in: people who are acting as caregivers for a sick family member. Frames were created to address the needs of people in different stages of the caregiving process (each coming with their own type of isolation and loneliness), focusing on subtle issues like the possibility for self-expression (the expression of identity that may be crushed through the pressure of constant care), the possible feelings of guilt that go along with such a care situation (caregivers often feel selfish when they do something to help themselves), and the realization that solutions should not have any feeling of obligation attached to them. The concrete interventions that were designed thus steered away from the conventional solutions of organizing events to distract and amuse the lonely, or bringing them together in groups to talk to each other so they won't be lonely. While these are all useful and honorable things to do, the Young Designers project moved on toward much more subtle approaches aimed at helping these caregivers to build up their own mental strength.

8 TRANSFORMATION

The Young Designers foundation and project partners (the Verwey-Jonker Institute and the Stichting DOEN) realize that this approach requires a new type of organization, one that doesn't try to "fix" loneliness through intervening in situations where loneliness occurs, but rather one that takes people on an important journey of learning and development. The working title of this fledgling initiative is the "Academy for Loneliness."

Please note that even within such very different frame creation projects, all nine steps of the frame creation process model (figure 4.1) should be addressed at some point to ensure a balanced outcome. But these varieties of frame creation projects also show that there is an inner strength and logic to the frame creation approach, a consistent quality that can be achieved in projects of many shapes and sizes. In chapter 7 we will delve deeper into the nature of frame creation as a way of thinking and acting, because the better we understand the core qualities of frame creation, the more flexible we can be in its application.

6 THE OPEN, COMPLEX, DYNAMIC, AND NETWORKED ORGANIZATION

DRIVING INNOVATION

The current interest in "design thinking" has been sparked by the trouble organizations have in dealing with today's open, complex, dynamic, and networked problem situations. Problematic situations arise when an organization's conventional problem-solving routines fail, when the equation

$$\text{WHAT} \quad + \quad \text{HOW} \quad \text{leads to} \quad \text{OUTCOME}$$

that an organization has been operating under breaks down. In these situations, it can be difficult to fathom what's wrong. Should the "what" be changed? But perhaps the "how" could also be inadequate, or the frame that drives the implication that a certain pattern of relationships will lead to the desired outcome could be faulty. Maybe the outcome itself, the desired value, is out of date because the organization has been misreading the developments in its societal context or the "market"?

The audio equipment manufacturer Bang and Olufsen, introduced in case study 2, is a perfect example of this predicament, as it experienced all of these questions in quick succession. Their capacity to innovate was honed to the periodical creation of new audio systems (the "what"), sometimes under pressure from the advent of new technologies, such as the CD as a carrier of digitized music (the "how"). Then the existing frame, the proposition that brilliance in sound and modernist aesthetics would satisfy its high-end customer base, came under pressure from the trend toward built-in audio systems. They subsequently reframed and sought ways to convey their sophisticated aesthetics through the customer's interaction with the (invisible) music source ("frame"). But while they were still experimenting with how they could deliver within this new frame, the desired functionality and value proposition changed. Music became a mobile, social medium, and the purist appetite for high audio quality waned (a shift in needs, demanding a new "outcome"). This shift meant that Bang and Olufsen had to reframe again, taking their quality brand away from interaction to become a service provider in the new music industry network (again a new "frame"). Bang and Olufsen's overcoming all of these problems in such a short period of time is exceptional; lesser companies would have given up a long time ago. Their experience illustrates that there are five different levels on which frame creation can be enlisted to drive innovation (see also Dorst 2011, and figure 6.1).

1   THE ROUTINE REACTION

Organizations often initially react to a change in their context in a way that requires the least effort and the fewest resources: they set out in a conventional problem-solving manner (through normal abduction; see chapter 3) to create a new "what" that will save the day while keeping the "how," the frame and the "outcome," constant. We have seen in the examples above that this is also often the face of the problem situation as it is first presented to a designer, implicitly framed by the client organization (Paton and Dorst 2011). This "staying within the frame" is seen as a good, low-risk strategy. It is the fallback position for many organizations. But taking this route is a strategic choice, like any other, and it should be done deliberately and thoughtfully, after a thorough analysis of the problem situation and its possible dynamics over time. Just sticking naively to this default strategy entails huge risks. The first lies in the fact that frames are full of assumptions about the way the world works. These assumptions can be deeply hidden in the discourse that sits behind the frame, and are thus engrained in the very terms that are used to think about the issues. This prestructures the problem situation—unquestioned frames can be complete thought worlds, with their own sense of rationality and a strong

THE ROUTINE REACTION

CONVENTIONAL PRACTICE

FRAME ADOPTION

FRAME CREATION PROJECTS

FRAME CREATION AS A CONTINUOUS PROCESS

Figure 6.1
Five levels of frame-based innovation.

ability to generate internal justifications. Solutions are considered to be "right" because they are conceived rationally within the frame, in a process of seemingly objective steps. Yet when a solution is "right" within the internal rationality of the frame, this doesn't mean that it is "right" in relation to the outside world. The second major risk of this strategy is the belief that sticking with routine responses will always be the most efficient way to tackle a problem situation. This is a real discussion stopper because nobody is against efficiency. But efficiency can be deceptive, because following this strategy can easily lead to ineffective measures being executed very efficiently. The third hazard of knee-jerk problem-solving is that by not reevaluating its own frame, the organization is also not scrutinizing the frames of competing players in the field. In this blinkered state, it could be overtaken by a competitor that has adopted a different approach. Routine problem-solving strategies work well only in a stable context, when we can trust that the existing frames and their accompanying scenarios are still effective.

2   CONVENTIONAL PRACTICE

If the normal abduction approach of creating a new "what" doesn't help, the organization may need to go into "design abduction" mode, which also requires them to create a new "how." The organization might simply use one of the other frames that it already has in its repertoire, in its internal "discourse." In doing so, it largely stays within its comfort zone and just applies a different existing practice to a specific case. The need to build a rich professional discourse to draw from is the reason designers often have material from old projects pinned to their office walls, as a constant peripheral-vision reminder of the frames and solutions they might want to build on in projects to come. Designers often draw on pretty far-flung associations and metaphors to enable the transfer of frames from one project to the next, imaginative bridges that enable the reuse of the old material within a new context. As discussed in chapter 3, leaders of design agencies spend a major amount of effort and time strategically elaborating on their repertoire of frames, making sure these frames are expressed and present in the practice of the firm, and that they are developed in a continuous evolution of the discourse. If this stack of frames is not shaken up periodically, the conventional practice of an organization might become hard to change.

3   FRAME ADOPTION

Alternatively, the organization might hire an external party that uses his or her experience to bring a new frame to the problematic situation. That frame could be employed by the organization for this particular project as a one-off application, or it might prove to be of significant worth and enter the organization's own discourse as an integral part of its problem-solving capability. When the frame becomes integrated in this way, it extends the problem-solving repertoire of the organization, and might be reapplied at a later date. This is often what designers and other external consultants hope for, because once a new frame has been successfully adopted and integrated, it becomes an avenue to extend the conversation with the organization to a strategic level. Adopting frames from outside parties is a key renewal strategy for organizations: the application of a new and different frame will lead to new experiences and, on reflection, to new lessons that can be learned. This is an important (though often implicit) learning mechanism for many organizations. But equally, the superficial adoption of an externally offered frame can be a strategy that keeps real change at bay, as the organization reaps the benefits from the one-off application of a new approach without having to renew its own discourse. This avoidance behavior can be incredibly effective: as a practicing designer, I have sometimes been amazed by how little was learned from what potentially could have been a groundbreaking project. To avoid being seen as a one-trick pony, the Designing Out Crime center always seeks to do multiple projects with a partner organization. These projects, all ostensibly aimed at direct on-the-ground results, create interesting new experiences that chip away at the partner organization's "old thinking" and reliance on current practices.

4   FRAME CREATION PROJECTS

This book has shown that a new frame can also be created from scratch, by going through a frame creation process. When such a process takes place within the organization itself, the new frame naturally becomes an integral part of that organization's discourse. This unconscious acceptance is a real advantage to placing the frame creation process within the organization as much as possible. Design research has shown that adopting a frame from outside the organization is tricky: frames cannot easily be transferred, as the frame not only needs to be communicated but also to be absorbed in a way that is actionable. In practical terms, this kind of active engagement means that the frame has to be reinvented by the receiving organization, and appropriated as its own idea. Compared to the level of "frame adoption," this is a much deeper process that directly impacts the practices of the organization, and potentially is an important driver for innovation. For this reason, both Young Designers and Designing Out Crime work in a strongly participatory manner. If an organization can come on board in the frame creation project as an equal partner and learner, this can lead to true frame innovation: the adoption of frame creation practices within the partner organization itself.

5   FRAME CREATION AS A CONTINUOUS PROCESS

The holy grail of frame creation is that the designerly ability to investigate themes and create new frames becomes embedded in the organization as a core skill and an almost continuous process. If this crucial step is taken, the organization will be able to better deal with any open, complex challenges it might face in the future. This frame innovation capacity involves the ongoing activity of monitoring the field for themes and exploring new themes that emerge, as well as the initiation of frame creation projects when the need arises. Over time, repeated frame creation can lead to an organization specializing in certain themes, and the ability to create frames that spring from these themes can become a very flexible basis for its identity.

TOWARD FRAME INNOVATION

Companies and government bodies alike are confronted by open, complex, dynamic, and networked problems—but they often do not realize it. Such problems initially do not look very different from any other issue that might come up. But when an organization finds itself confronted with an endless parade of similar incidents, alarm bells should be ringing that something more fundamental has shifted and its current frames are not good enough anymore.

For example, the police are under pressure because as soon as they intervene in a public space (e.g., ending a brawl), there will be at least ten people with their smartphones out, filming the scene—the police are then operating in the middle of an open, complex, dynamic, and networked problem situation. The open and networked nature of the problem situation means that there is no margin for error, and they will be held to account if the situation gets out of hand. The police know only too well that they are living in the spotlight now; if something goes wrong, the video clips will be all over the Web, sparking the inevitable outcry in the media. As a response, the knee-jerk reaction from the authorities is to create more rules that will prevent this particular type of unfortunate incident from happening again. The result is that the sheer number of rules of engagement that a police officer must adhere to is way beyond what is practical, and far beyond what a police officer can keep in mind—let alone act upon quickly in a crisis situation. But the police know for sure that disgruntled people will use these rules to hound them, after the fact. So creating all these rules is not only nonsensical (we can never foresee and prevent every detail of every problematic situation that might occur), it is also actively harmful: police officers should have the freedom to improvise, based on a keen understanding of their role and the outcomes they should achieve. This illustrates the interesting phenomenon that while the world is becoming more *dynamic*, the direct reaction of most organizations is to seize up and become more *static* in an effort to control the situation. A vicious circle begins, leading to autism and a reinforced addiction to solving problems by relying on rules. This development takes an organization away from the original core problem (the fact that the world is becoming more open, complex, dynamic, and networked) in exactly the opposite direction. That is disastrous. We see this all the time, in all walks of life: organizations becoming very defensive and protective in the face of problems they do not understand, stumbling from incident to incident while holding on to their old frames and rationalities (Boutellier 2013). But how can one avoid such an inappropriate reaction, when the knee-jerk reaction is quite understandable and initially seems the reasonable thing to do? The answer lies at a structural level. An organization that needs to tackle these open, complex, dynamic, and networked problems will effectively have to become open, complex, dynamic, and networked in its own processes, structure, and organizational culture. This is a formidable challenge because organizations are, by definition, established to create order and tend to stasis. The million-dollar question is: "How can an organization become more open, complex, dynamic, and networked without descending into chaos?"

The fear of losing control runs very deep (remember the "rational high ground" syndrome from chapter 1). The frame creation approach leads to an alternative practice that allows us to deal with complex realities in layers and at its deepest level, that of themes, offers a respite. These themes are stable, and a deep understanding of them allows an organization to deal thoughtfully with the chaotic and messy everyday incidents from a stable core. The possibility of being simultaneously flexible in daily action and well-grounded at the root is a key quality that frame innovation can offer organizations. Not only will an organization that has adopted frame innovation become more nimble and resilient in dealing with challenges, it can become proactive in building an understanding of the themes that lie underneath the problems that reality throws up. An organization that monitors the themes in its environment is ready to create frames and move to action when needed. For instance, a housing authority that understands, on a deep theme level, teenagers' process of identity formation will be more flexible in its responses when a problem arises (say, when a group of loitering teens causes trouble in a neighborhood).

This familiarity can engender a fundamental confidence that the organization can deal with any problem that arises. A frame-innovating organization should constantly be investigating the themes in the broad area that touches upon its operations, scouting out for developments that may give rise to new problems or possibilities. This cuts to the core of the matter: a basic issue with conventional problem-solving methods is that they require a problem to start with. An active, really proactive organization should be able to develop new "solutions" before the problems even arise or get the chance to develop into full-blown crises. That is the more profound promise of becoming a frame innovator: existing in the world in this way, relating to the world in this way fosters a less nervous, problem-prone existence. With such fearlessness and confidence comes the possibility of adopting a truly long-term perspective and assigning a healthy relativity to short-term issues, incidents, and the crises of the day. It is this confidence that creates space, allowing the organization to completely bypass the age-old syndromes discussed in chapter 1 in one fell swoop. An assured organization will be more open to collaboration, less prone to oversimplify and overrationalize a problem, more flexible in its problem approach, quicker to adapt to changing circumstances, and less preoccupied with conserving a precious identity that is anchored in past performance. The syndromes are all short-term defensive mechanisms that are, in the end, driven by fear and a need to cling to a feeling of control in a fluid and changing world.

Many people in organizations will understand this and agree that the frame creation approach makes absolute sense—but that realization doesn't make it easy for them to become frame innovators in their organizations. As a process, skillset, and mentality, frame innovation is completely incompatible with conventional organizational processes and structures. The Young Designers foundation and the Designing Out Crime center have to deal with the fact that their practices don't integrate easily with the practices of their partner organizations. The old thinking and syndromes that were listed in the first chapter can be deeply engrained; old habits don't die easily, even in the face of a better alternative. While YD/ and DOC like to see themselves as catalysts for radical innovation, they find themselves to be unwilling revolutionaries, using guerrilla tactics to undermine old structures. Creating an organizational context for frame innovation is a huge challenge, and the jury is still out on which strategies are successful, under which circumstances. But examples are trickling in.

CASE 17
Reframing the city at night:
On a new understanding of public space

The City of Sydney has been proactively engaged with the follow-up on the Kings Cross entertainment district project (see case 8). After that experience, the city council felt inspired by the realization that it is possible to change the dynamics of the city at night in a positive way—and not just in Kings Cross. They set up an extensive study of nightlife throughout the council area, which resulted in very detailed maps of who is where at what time at night (by various methods, such as counting pedestrians). Advice was sought from other cities about their strategies for creating a lively and vibrant nighttime economy. After a lengthy ideation and consultation process, various frames were created and almost 200 concrete measures proposed. One of the key frames was triggered by the realization that presently, only 6 percent of the people out on the streets of the central business district at 11 p.m. are over 40 years old. Office workers were leaving the city district after working hours, when the area was taken over by youth on a massive scale—resulting in problems with public order and alcohol-related incidents. Part of the strategy now is to keep a much more varied population in the city at night. Proposed measures include the extension of shop closing hours (making it possible to shop after work) and restaurant closing hours (to get a good meal afterward), the introduction of high-quality food carts (in particular for concert and theater goers), and stimulating employers to allow flexible work hours.

In this example, the frame creation project has been scaled up to extend its influence on the structures and processes of the organization. Now we will examine a case study where the need to create an organization that can establish its own frames is confronted head-on, without earlier frame creation projects to build from.

CASE 18
Reframing a design school:
Educating for a changing profession

The starting point for the transformation process at this design school was not a specific issue or emergency: the school is well respected in the field and provides a thorough and solid grounding in design to its students. The spark that kindled change was the worldwide movement of design into academia, which has led to intense soul-searching about the meaning and content of "design at an academic level" (Dorst 2013a). The new academic designer is able to deal with more complex problems than the traditional skills-based design paradigms allow—as a result, academic design moves away from teaching a skills base (the typical "design ability" [Cross 1990] approach) to a knowledge base, extending its scope, its breadth of application, and its intellectual depth. Pioneering design schools have adopted such an academic design profile, and their graduates successfully operate in positions that hitherto would not have been accessible to designers. But setting out to change the very nature of the profession that is being taught is a big step for a school, and is a formidable challenge for both staff and students. Even the perception of what signifies "quality" in a designer will have to shift. To radically transform the practice of an organization as complex as an educational institution, we need to be active on many fronts— changing the discourse, very much like the leading designers that were introduced at the end of chapter 3. New staff members have been hired that embody various aspects of academic design—some of them more research-oriented, others crossing boundaries between disciplines. In parallel to these bringers of new practices, people have been hired who create critical frameworks (scholars in critical theory, history, and social sciences) to reflect on these new developments and help shape them. Talks and exhibitions have been organized to stimulate debate. New research labs have been set up in prominent places to highlight the research activity going on inside. A research gallery has been opened, showing results of both theory-based and practice-led research projects. Within the curriculum, multidisciplinary design labs have been established where students learn how to deal with open-ended challenges outside their disciplinary comfort zone. Exhibitions become a regular feature of various courses, showing their development and exposing staff and students to discussion and debate.

What can we learn from these cases? First, it's clear that changing an organization's practice is a curiously indirect process. A practice is a complex combination of perceptions, thoughts, and actions that are inextricably linked (Bower, Crabtree, and Keogh 1996). Because practices touch every aspect of an organization, the changing of a practice involves many small initiatives, rather than expressing a grand vision and expecting people to fall in line behind the visionary leader. In the case of the design school, these initiatives involved human resources, the execution of demonstration projects, and making these new developments visible (through physical changes to the building). We can only be certain that a new practice has taken root when its three elements (seeing, thinking, and doing) have been implemented, a feedback mechanism kicks in (when new doing leads to new seeing and thinking, and so on), and the practice reinforces itself.

As it is our aim for frame creation to become an influential new practice within organizations, we will have to confront head-on the "mismatch" between frame innovation and the organizations' normal ways of working. We will do so in the next chapter.

7 THE THREE CHALLENGES OF FRAME INNOVATION

I hope to have convinced you that frame creation is a much-needed extension of the repertoire of problem-solving approaches available to us, as it creates a whole new way to address problems and capture opportunities. But despite its obvious qualities, the adoption of frame creation, and its embedding in organizations as a frame innovation practice, is not always easy—the very features that make frame creation such a valuable new practice also make it hard to get individuals and organizations to adopt it. Frame innovation is at right angles to current problem-solving and innovation practices: it entails a huge and fundamental shift in how people and organizations see a problem, how they think about it, and what they do to address it.

This rift between frame creation and current practices leads to many practical problems in the adoption of frame creation and the establishment of a frame innovation practice; these will be addressed in some final words of advice in the next chapter. Solutions to many of these issues have already been built into the frame creation approach itself, based on the rich experience gathered through more than ten years of experimental projects. But it would be wrong to assume that the barriers to frame creation are nothing more than practical implementation problems. They are the result of much more fundamental differences that will never disappear. These fundamental issues need to be acknowledged and understood well—at least understanding the misunderstandings that can occur is a first step toward finding a way to deal with them. How does frame creation differ from conventional approaches? At the core of the frame creation approach are three ways in which a frame creation practice moves away from what people are used to and expect, and thus three ways in which frame creation clashes with current practice. These challenges are located in the realms of "seeing" (our perception of the world is organized by solutions, rather than problems), "thinking" (the world is used to a static notion of "rationality"), and "doing" (the world has set ways of dealing with novelty and innovation). Frame creation is seeing, thinking, and doing things differently from before—let's now reflect on these differences and map the challenges that lie ahead when we set out on the path of implementing the frame creation approach and internalizing it—as frame innovation—into the ways of working of an organization.

SEEING DIFFERENTLY

Frame creation entails a shift in perception, seeing the problem situation differently than before. This is problematic because the problem-solving capacity in our society is implicitly organized by type of solution, rather than by type of problem. The professions we are in, and the roles we define in organizations, are defined by a discourse and a worldview that inadvertently push us in the direction of predetermined solutions. When you hold a hammer, everything looks like a nail, as the saying goes. So, confronted with a complex and messy problem situation, we all see it from different angles depending on where we come from. We have seen time and again in the case studies throughout this book that complex problems can be described in many different ways, and each description implies a solution. For instance, of course the police would see the problems in the Kings Cross entertainment district as a crime issue; of course the City of Sydney would see the same Kings Cross situation as a problem of public space design, and so on. And these could all be valid analyses of aspects of the problem. But these perspectives all come with their own solutions, and taken separately they may hold only part of the key to success. For this reason, these organizations should sit down together and work in multidisciplinary teams: by putting many different (professional) worldviews together, they may hope to create solutions in which all their insights and qualities are combined.

By contrast, frame creation is not focused on combining the solution directions in this way; instead, it steps back from the simplifications that come from these professional perspectives in order to delve deeply into the complexity of the problem field and create themes that are "neutral," in the sense that they don't presuppose a discipline to solve the issue. In the first five phases of the frame creation model, frame creation is staunchly problem-focused, and steers away from making any assumptions on the nature or type of solution. The type of solution begins to surface in the next step, when frames are proposed as paths to a solution. That is also when the disciplinary approaches become relevant again. Some of the people and parties involved in a frame creation process may have a hard time grasping this approach. They will have a strong, inadvertent tendency to revert back to disciplinary thinking, and jump to conclusions. As we will see in the next chapter, this can derail a frame creation process, and lead to less than interesting results. All stakeholders and participants in a frame creation project will inevitably come to the process with their own approaches and built-in solutions, and they need to be coerced out of that comfort zone toward a new openness. Managing the frame creation process in such a way that it remains "profession-neutral" requires great skill on the part of the project leader.

THINKING DIFFERENTLY

Frame creation is not just seeing things differently; it is also a different way of thinking. There is a logic behind frame creation, but it is a different kind of logic than the one that people and organizations are used to. Understanding the underlying logic of the frame creation approach starts with understanding the central notion of "a frame." We have seen that frames have a dual nature: they include both an approach to the problem situation and the proposing of a solution direction. It is precisely through this duality that frames can act as a bridge between the world of values and needs, and the world of real action. To take case study 8 as an example: the Designing Out Crime team looked at the Kings Cross entertainment area in Sydney *as if* it was not a crime problem but an entertainment problem (thus proposing a new approach), and the central frame of the music festival then indicated many avenues for creating solutions. *If* this is a music festival, *then* people should be able to come and go; *if* this is a music festival, *then* people should be able to be entertained away from the main attractions; *if* this is a music festival, *then* people should be provided with information to help them find their preferred entertainment option; and so on. The dual nature of frames informs the logic and structure of the frame creation process model: the main emphasis in the process shifts from "approaching the problem" (steps 1–4) to the critical investigation of possible solution directions (in steps 6, 7, and 8).

The first two steps in the frame creation process, which concentrate on the problem as presented, are necessary because frames are intrinsic—we cannot formulate or approach a problem without framing it. We cannot *not* have a frame. The implicit framing of the problem situation needs to be investigated; it is vitally important to understand the frame that led to the occurrence of the problem situation in the first place. The initial framing could originate in the history of the problem, it could be a general cultural convention (e.g., the close link between "care" and "control" in the health system [case 6]), or it could stem from the interaction between the problem owner and the inner ring of stakeholders. Beyond that core group is the wider field of parties who have not participated in the problem situation before but who have a potential influence, and could develop a direct interest in the problem if it were framed in a different way. In the frame creation approach, the search for new frames is shaped by the need to shed the preconceptions of existing frames. By moving to the outer rim of the field and analyzing the shared themes in the broader problem arena, such new approaches are allowed to emerge. From that moment, the process flips to concentrating on the second nature of the frame and becomes a critical creative exploration of possibilities—applying creative forward-thinking to spot possibilities, while exercising a keen critical judgment in the performance of repeated reality checks. We can then reengage with the inner ring of stakeholders and the problem owner to present them with possible future scenarios that resolve the original problem situation. All elements of the original problem situation are first questioned and then redefined in the frame creation process, step by step—as expressed in the nested-circles model (see figure 7.1).

This model defines the inner logic of the frame creation approach, and should engender trust in the sequence of steps in the frame creation process model. The frame creation approach is consistent and coherent; it is not a cheap trick based on some superficial techniques that designers have dreamt up, but a serious approach to problem-solving that provides an interesting alternative to conventional problem-solving.

However, to really understand the difference between frame creation and conventional problem-solving, we need to delve a little deeper into the assumptions that underlie conventional problem-solving, especially the key concept of "rationality." Rationality is considered the bedrock of critical discussion and successful action. This is a cultural "given" that runs very deep in our veins: we are used to the convention that we must be able to give an account of our thoughts and actions using rational arguments. We aspire to

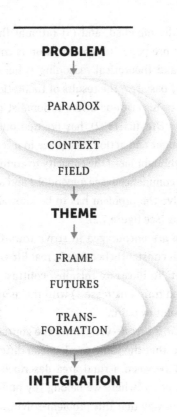

PROBLEM
↓
PARADOX

CONTEXT

FIELD
↓
THEME
↓
FRAME

FUTURES

TRANS-
FORMATION
↓
INTEGRATION

Figure 7.1
Frame creation as zooming out and concentrating.

be seen as a "reasonable" person. Straying from the narrow path of rationality is "not normal," and while some groups (such as artists) can get away with it to some extent (as cultural court jesters), a perceived lack of rationality sets a person apart from polite society. Irrational people are outcasts who cannot be tolerated. The veneration of rationality that underpins our view of the world has been critically investigated by George Lakoff and Mark Johnson in their groundbreaking book *Philosophy in the Flesh* (1999). They list five key assumptions behind what they call the "theory of rational action": (1) rational thought is literal, (2) rational thought is logical, (3) rational thought is conscious, (4) rational thought is disembodied, and (5) rational thought is dispassionate. Later they add one more point: (6) a distinction is commonly made between practical reasoning and theoretical reasoning (where we hold that rational action must be firmly based on the results of theoretical rather than practical reasoning). Dreyfus, in his critique of the rationalist paradigm in the field of artificial intelligence (Dreyfus 1992), has pointed out an additional assumption: (7) rational thought and action take place in a "closed world." By this he means that rational thought lacks the capacity to admit new information once problem-solving has commenced (see appendix 2 and Simon 1973): everything that is needed to solve the problem has to be knowable before the problem-solving process begins (see figure 7.2).

In our society, we are encouraged to strive toward realizing this ideal of rationality. Yet we fail constantly because in real life these seven assumptions are almost never met. To illustrate this, just contrast the real-life process of planning a high-speed train link (case 1) with the assumptions of the "theory of rational action," point by point.

(1) *Rational thought is literal*—yet, within the context of planning the high-speed train, it is clear that the same words mean different things to different people. The contrast between a rural area described as "uninteresting" (by one of the planners) or as "where we belong" by one of the locals could not be greater. There is no way that this problem-solving process can be built on a common ground of literal concepts. (2) *Rational thought is logical*—but it is clear that the assumptions of the various stakeholders which form the basis of their own "logic" are very dissimilar. There is no dominant or overarching logic in this problem arena, so people will try to impose their own version on others. This is power play: the ones who can dictate the terms and metaphors that lead the discussion are sure to get their way. (3) *Rational thought is conscious*—but many stakeholders who need to be taken into account actually will not be conscious of their own standpoint, assumptions, and preconceptions. Even professional organizations like the government, which tend to claim they have rationality on their side, rarely know their own motivations and preconceptions. (4) *Rational thought is disembodied*—this assumption doesn't hold either. The people living around the projected track initially felt in shock, nervous, and sick to the stomach, and their anger rose as the consultation process unfolded and they felt ignored. As a result, they lacked the capacity to have empathy for other stakeholders or to contribute to the resolution of the problem. (5) *Rational thought is dispassionate*—none of the parties in this problem arena can

RATIONAL THOUGHT IS **LITERAL**

RATIONAL THOUGHT IS **LOGICAL**

RATIONAL THOUGHT IS **CONSCIOUS**

RATIONAL THOUGHT IS **DISEMBODIED**

RATIONAL THOUGHT IS **DISPASSIONATE**

THEORY LEADS PRACTICE

RATIONAL **ACTION** TAKES PLACE IN A **CLOSED WORLD**

Figure 7.2
The assumptions behind rational thought.

be called dispassionate. Even the civil servants, whose personal distance to the issues was probably the greatest of all stakeholders, got caught up in the emotional and personal impact of the process and groupthink. Their assumptions and power structures were challenged, and they felt threatened. (6) *Theory leads practice*—this may have been true initially (in an esoteric planning stage, before the discussions started), but soon the very practical nature of the problem took over. From that moment, all stakeholders were thrown into the situation, and not only did the individual parties lose sight of the overview, they actively chose to work from a limited understanding of the broader situation. (7) *Rational action takes place in a closed world*—this has never been a closed or contained problem arena. System borders changed, new information came in all the time, the learning processes of all the various parties drove the development of new standpoints, coalitions of convenience between stakeholders were created and died, etc.

This analysis shows that the problem situation badly fails all the assumptions that are needed for a rationalistic approach. Yet that approach was followed, as the problem owner felt there was no other choice. The cracks in the ensuing problem-solving process were not due to incompetence or to certain stakeholders being "difficult"—they run much deeper than that: the problem-solving process itself was fundamentally flawed (this case will be continued in chapter 8). The realization that these seven prerequisites for rational action are obviously unrealistic assumptions for most if not all real-life problem situations has led to the creation of a distinction between "theoretical reasoning" and "practical reasoning." While "theoretical reasoning" strictly adheres to the seven assumptions, "practical reasoning" is more lenient, in that it accepts that we are limited by "bounded rationality" in our decision-making—purely because our poor brains run out of information-processing capacity as soon as we have to hold more than "seven plus or minus two" chunks of information in our heads simultaneously (Newell and Simon 1972). But this fact doesn't lift the burden of being literal, logical, conscious, disembodied, and dispassionate in our thoughts.

Perhaps we should see this view of rationality as an ideal and use it as a beacon, knowing that we will seldom achieve it. And perhaps we should be content with our incomplete attempts to prerationalize our actions (in an effort to be strategic) and our use of rationality after the fact to justify decisions we have arrived at by other means (postrationalization). But what could those "other means" be? How can we think and make decisions, if not through rational reasoning? The Dutch writer Van Zomeren likened his own thinking process to a colony of chipmunks: thoughts pop up in unexpected places, disappearing just as quickly (Van Zomeren 2000). Poet and writer Robert Graves has similarly described poetic intuition in his essay "The Case for Xanthippe." Xanthippe was the wife of Socrates, and was portrayed by Plato as bad-tempered, bossy, and unreasonable. Yet Graves sees her as an emotional and practical thinker, and the necessary antidote to the overrationalization of Socrates and his circle (Graves 1991). Heidegger, in turn, has described how being "thrown" into a situation limits our ability to use our capacity to reason rationally (Heidegger 1962; Winograd and Flores 1986). One of his examples is the position we operate from when participating in a meeting: our situation is characterized by a limited overview of the issues, a limited capacity to influence the direction of the discussion, and the vexed problem that saying nothing is also an act that affects the situation. Heidegger uses this example to highlight how, in this moment of the eternal now, we continuously improvise based on experience, habit, a sense of a pattern, gut feeling, and our drive to move in a certain direction. Then we postrationalize and create stories to support the myth of our rational reasoning.

This could lead to problems, though, because theories and models are not only used to describe reality, but they also shape our perception of it (they change our "seeing"). Then there is a risk that reality will be manipulated to fit the theory, instead of the other way around (as in the Greek myth of Procrustes, the innkeeper who had one size of bed and would stretch the unlucky short traveler until he fit in it or, in the case of a tall guest, would chop off the parts that stuck out). In fact, this is the fate that normally befalls the open, complex, dynamic, and networked problems: they are subjected to a rational simplification, limited and adapted to what the organization can handle, instead of the organization developing itself to the point where it can deal with these complex issues as they are. The case study of the high-speed train link illustrates how even a sophisticated organization like the Dutch government fights the nature of the problem instead of accepting it. In a sense, the first three syndromes that we mentioned in chapter 1—the "lone warrior," "freeze the world," and "self-made box"—can all be shown to result from the limited view of rationality that underlies the actions of these organizations, and from their inability to reimagine their practices in the face of open, complex, dynamic, and networked problems. This inability is caused by the fourth syndrome: the people and organizations that were introduced in the case studies of chapter 1 were fearful of leaving their "rational high ground." They imagine that beyond this high ground there is only quicksand, so they had better stay up above. But the train case study shows that this will not do, and that we need to come up with an alternative to the restrictive notion of rationality that underlies much of conventional problem-solving. Frame creation offers elements of such a different, more fluid rationality.

To consider whether frame creation really contains the elements of an alternative to conventional problem-solving through the creation of a more fluid rationality, we will now briefly contrast the seven central assumptions underpinning the theory of rational action with the principles of frame creation. While in the theory of rational action (1) *rational thought is literal*, in frame creation the same words mean different things to different people, and so metaphor is a driving force in many of the creative steps. And in rational action, (2) *rational thought is considered to be logical*. We have already seen that there is an inner logic to the frame creation process, but we have also seen that in applying this process, the assumptions of the different stakeholders form the basis of their own "rationality." There is no a priori dominant or overarching logic for looking at the problem situation—the core of the frame creation process is the creation of such a logic through theme analysis and framing. Where rational thought and frame creation are largely in line is in the aim (3) *to make thoughts conscious*. But from the outset, frame creation accepts the fact that many stakeholders will not be conscious of their own standpoints, assumptions, and preconceptions. This is where frame creation seeks to make thoughts and assumptions explicit to trigger inspiration and reflection. There is a significant difference in that the theory of rational action sees (4) *rational thought as disembodied*, while one of the core processes in frame creation, the phenomenological analysis that produces themes, is largely based on empathy and the ability to understand the lived experience of the parties in the broader problem arena. That is how deep understanding is achieved, and deeper layers of meaning are brought to the surface. While (5) *rational thought is dispassionate*, frame creation is engaged, is guided by empathy, and employs personal experience in the sense-making and creative phases. Yet another difference is that whereas in rational action (6) *theory leads practice*, in frame creation every premise about how the world might work is suspended, and the practices of the stakeholders and parties in the field are what lead to the formation of a "theory," a frame hypothesis, which is then critically examined. (7) *Rational action takes place in a closed world*, while frame creation extends beyond the problem owner and the inner ring of stakeholders, opening up to be informed by the multiple sources in the broader field. In the later stages, the information generated in the frame creation process (like proposed themes and frames, business plans, and the like) becomes a dominant force steering the process.

We can conclude that the differences between the frame creation approach and the conventional theory of rational action are huge. Yet there is nothing irrational or random about the careful sequence of steps that make up the frame creation approach, and in many ways it shares the values that underlie the rationalist approach. Frame creation is as concerned with clarity and inner consistency as conventional problem-solving, for the frame creation approach contains extensive checks and balances to verify the realism and validity of the frames proposed. But frame creation (and other design-based approaches that may be developed as its siblings) could be seen as a first step toward creating more fluent approaches to rationality. There may be quicksand and chaos beyond the rational high ground, but thoughtful and logical approaches can be developed to help us traverse that terrain. This does, however, require the problem solver to embrace the open, complex, dynamic, and networked nature of the problem instead of denying it.

DOING DIFFERENTLY

In chapter 6 we saw that the originality of the frame creation approach extends beyond "seeing" and "thinking" to also sparking a new approach to achieving novelty in organizations, "frame innovation." To understand the ways in which the frame creation approach is new, and the extent to which it differs from conventional ways of dealing with innovation, we first have to delve into the domain of the management sciences, and particularly into the field of innovation management.

The core paradox of innovation management lies in the fact that the ideal image of an organization still is that of a well-oiled machine where efficiency reigns supreme. The need to create novelty is at odds with this model, as novelty inevitably disturbs existing processes and might be accompanied by "creative destruction." How do we find a balance between routine operation and the need for novelty and change in an organization? To answer this question, the field of innovation management has had to become a hybrid: it combines a rich mix of subjects in policy-making, strategy formulation, organizational structures, and management styles with elements of design theory (notably, creative problem-solving; see van der Lugt 2001) and fundamental analyses of the notion of innovation itself. Combined, these create a context for thinking about innovation within organizations. Lately, design has come to be seen as a potential driver of strategic innovation in the organization (Verganti 2009). In pursuing these goals, the field of innovation management has developed ways to stimulate innovation while maintaining a strong connection with the "planning and control" paradigm that is so dominant in management science, in many business schools, and within organizations. Most thinkers in innovation management have found a way around the fundamental paradox of stability versus dynamism by concentrating innovation and encapsulating it in analytical steps. The achievement of novelty in a "creative phase" ("idea generation") is restricted by the determination of goals and criteria in the step before it, and the evaluation in the step that follows it. This clever isolation of creative steps within a rationalist process has been very successful. Yet the frame creation approach gives us a different perspective on novelty and the way it could be embedded in organizations, potentially leading to significantly different processes and structures. Let's take some of the key notions in the field of innovation, and briefly explore the differences between how these are defined and dealt with in innovation management and in frame innovation (figure 7.3), to discover where these very different approaches can complement each other.

KINDS OF NOVELTY
While innovation management tends to look for novelty through the generation of innovative and interesting solutions, frame creation is squarely focused on problems, seeking novelty through the development of a new approach to the problem situation. Innovation management tends to stress the generative

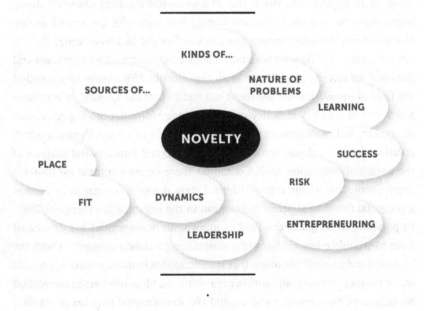

Figure 7.3
Aspects of novelty in relation to organizations.

aspect of creativity as embodied in techniques like brainstorming, using "creative sessions" to create a wide spread of associations and ideas to be clustered and evaluated. This approach is in marked contrast to the problem-oriented, explorative, targeted creativity that can be observed in expert designers and that has become one of the principles of frame creation.

SOURCES OF NOVELTY

One of the key paradoxes underlying innovation management thinking is the problem of judging novelty when the criteria by which we judge are still set according to the original framing of the problem. Frame creation sidesteps this paradox by focusing on a reconsideration of the original problem situation before generating solutions. In innovation management, sources of novel solutions are typically sought through methods like the SWOT analysis (in a strengths, weaknesses, opportunities, and threats analysis, the internal strengths and weaknesses of an organization are compared to the external opportunities and threats to determine what would be fruitful future directions for the organization). Such a SWOT analysis maps the organization and its context—thus, the novelty might be limited by the organization as is and its original view of the relevant context. And, from a frame creation perspective, we would argue that the words used to describe these strengths, weaknesses, opportunities, and threats are part of specific frames, which need to be examined before such an analysis can be done. Otherwise, the use of these words could limit the scope of the analysis in unforeseen ways. In frame creation, the source of novelty lies in the exploration of a broader field and the emergence of themes.

THE PLACE OF NOVELTY IN ORGANIZATIONS

As described above, innovation management tends to nurture and protect the innovative capacity in an organization by placing it in relative isolation from other organizational processes. In frame creation, novelty comes from themes that are universal by their very nature and may exist throughout an organization, in distributed actor networks. Because it relegates creativity to specific brief phases in the larger innovation process, innovation management does not address the fundamental paradox between stability and change. It sidesteps this paradox in the time (process) dimension by creating a special isolated "creative phase," or in the organizational dimension by relegating the responsibility for novelty to a "product champion" who has to carry the new idea through to completion, while withstanding all attacks from within the innovation-adverse organization. Sometimes the sidestepping also has a physical nature, as when organizations create "skunk works": offsite innovation initiatives where the normal rules of the organization do not apply.

OPEN, COMPLEX, DYNAMIC, AND NETWORKED PROBLEMS
The open, complex, dynamic, and networked problems and the organizational syndromes that they highlight have been addressed by innovation management literature in various ways, as exemplified by the models and methods of multidisciplinary innovation and open innovation. With the introduction of the frame creation approach, this book has offered an alternative way of dealing with these problems, through the adoption of a set of strong and coherent design practices. Frame creation imports a set of sophisticated practices from a discipline that has been versed in the creation of new solutions. In comparison, some innovation management methods seem to be reactive to the syndromes in the life of our organizations, compensating (and often overcompensating) for a perceived problem: for example, they propose that companies are too closed in their outlook, and need to think about "open innovation" (which runs the risk of opening the doors much too widely, leading straight to chaos).

THE CONTEXT
For dealing with the dynamic nature of the context, innovation management proposes sophisticated methods for tracking and analyzing change (market research, trend watching, forecasting, scenario methods, etc.). One of the key features of frame creation is that it seeks to look beyond the restless changes of the day and base its new approaches on the universality and stability of the themes. Both are needed, in the end: this is surely a point where innovation management and frame innovation can complement each other.

DEFINITION OF SUCCESS
The definition of success in innovation management tends to be taken from the general management literature, where short-term pressures (return on investment, or ROI, and shareholder value) often prevail. Frame creation is quite radical in that it takes a long-term perspective. Although that could be perceived as a weakness of the frame creation approach in this fast-moving and restless world, it may actually be a much closer reflection of good management practice in the real world. In a delightful study, Hart (1996) has shown that the

prevalent measure of "success" that is used in marketing to select "best practices" to study and emulate does not correspond with what managers in the
field consider "successful" projects. The marketing measure of success is based
on financial criteria like return on investment, while the managers were much
more interested in projects that maybe had not been so profitable but had provided a learning experience on which future financial success could be built.
They were not very interested in the high-yielding "cash cow" projects that the
management scientists had considered to be best practices and encouraged us
to emulate.

RISK
Innovation management doesn't shy away from the risk that is part and parcel
of innovation, and celebrates the abilities and personal attributes of innovation leaders who take risks. Perhaps the high mortality rate among innovative
projects gives rise to a culture of admiring these "project champions" and cel-
ebrating the innovator who perseveres against all odds—and other such highly
charged battle metaphors. In contrast, frame creation is decidedly undramatic:
the risk that is inherent in the creation of newness is reduced enormously by
the careful analysis and the creative exploration that make up the frame creation process. Yet most of the cases described in this book have been seen as
both radical and successful projects by the partner organizations. On reflection,
one could posit that the restless jumping toward ideas that is seen as inevitable in most innovation management literature is what introduces risk into
the innovation process—a risk that is then accepted as part of the heroics of
innovation leadership. It is worth considering whether some of this risk may
be self-inflicted and unnecessary. If I owned shares in a company, I would be
more comfortable with a firm that uses the frame creation approach to achieving radical innovation than with a firm that exposes itself to unnecessary risks.

INNOVATION LEADERSHIP
This raises interesting questions on the "culture" of the fields of innovation
management and frame creation. We know that professional cultures are
closely related to the way we solve problems in our social group ("community of practice"). Whereas innovation management, which has its roots in
U.S. business schools, stresses radical innovation, risk, and leadership, (often
expressed in terms of military metaphors), frame creation is more deliberate, a
trait that might betray its origin in mainland Europe. The depth of the frame

creation approach cuts out risk while still achieving radical innovation—but by eliminating risk, it also rules out the opportunity to be a hero in the classic sense of the word. Frame creation might be more amenable to, say, the Indian or Chinese approaches to issues—see appendix 4. These cultural factors might also explain why, while the model is very widely applicable, frame creation has found its first experimental platforms in the public sector. Private-sector companies have been slower in realizing its potential and embracing the possibilities of frame creation. One could speculate that this is because the culture behind the frame creation approach doesn't come naturally to them, and they do not have the processes and structures in their organizations to deal with this type of innovation. But examples like the department store case study (case 12) have shown that the depth of the frame creation approach is not wasted on the commercial sector.

ENTREPRENEURING

A clear contact point between the frame creation approach and the thinking in the broader field of management and organizational sciences lies in the area of entrepreneuring. This field has lately become more dynamic in its approach as it has turned away from studying the personality traits of great entrepreneurs (and glorifying these innovation leaders as "lone warriors") to concentrate on the study of processes. Hence the word "entrepreneuring," rather than "entrepreneurship" (Steyaert 2007). With this shift in focus, the debate has moved away from discussions of nature versus nurture (can entrepreneurship be taught, or is it an innate personality trait?) and toward the fruitful bringing together of many theories and viewpoints on the practices of these entrepreneurs. A new richness in the field has resulted. The theory of effectuation is an attempt to come up with such a central model; it finds its roots in the same logical schemas that were used in chapter 3 to position design reasoning relative to the other reasoning modes. In "effectuation," the central reasoning mode of entrepreneurial thinking is characterized as an "even if ..." reasoning pattern that deals first and foremost with issues of possibility and risk (Sarasvathy 2008). This theoretical basis is now matched to real-world entrepreneurial practices by studying entrepreneurial people. These studies are performed in much the same way that designers have been studied, using protocol analysis of individuals and groups in laboratory and real-life situations (see appendix 1 for an example). The patterns of thinking found are interestingly similar too. As it is, the lessons learned from these rich data sets are restricted by the adherence of the entrepreneuring scholars to Herbert Simon's theories—entrepreneurial activity is thus seen through the rather limiting lens of rational problem-solving. Notions like interpretation and framing do not come into this yet, but given the direction we have taken in this book, one can easily see where connections can be made. Frame innovation is a key entrepreneurial activity.

To conclude, there is much that can be learned from innovation management, and the field has contributed enormously to the innovative capacity of organizations. It has flagged many problems that are very real in practice, reflected upon them, and proposed avenues of solution that are very relevant. It has also provided a context for innovation in organizations. However, in its modeling of innovation, the field of innovation management has adapted to the "manufacturing" type of organization as it has developed in the industrial economy (Smulders 2006), and many of the critical remarks above stem from the difficulties that arise from the compromises that accompany this adaptation. Frame creation is, in a sense, more radical in that it steps away from that image of an organization and takes its inspiration from the knowledge economy. But this means that frame creation often doesn't fit easily in the existing processes of organizations that are structured along the principles of the industrial economy. While this is a deep and fundamental difference that as such cannot be resolved, some key frame creation tools and practices have been developed to traverse this terrain. They will be introduced in the next chapter.

8 THE ART OF FRAME INNOVATION

MAKING IT HAPPEN

Frame creation is a situated process that requires new thinking every time. So there will never be a "recipe," a set of actions that can be followed more or less thoughtlessly, by anyone, at any moment, and that will lead to good results (Suchman 1987). This book therefore seeks to deliver the next best thing: a keen understanding of the principles and practices of frame creation that will help the practitioner to be thoughtful and flexible in achieving radical innovation. If anything, this book is a do-it-yourself manual rather than a how-to guide. This final chapter will look at some of the key lessons learned over the years of applying frame creation in various contexts, and will support readers with practical advice to take away on their path to integrating frame creation practices in their ways of working, and becoming frame innovators in their own right. But first, let's bring back the practice perspective through an extensive case study, described in terms of the nine-step frame creation model. Critical moments in this process will be used to illustrate the advice, tools, and methods that follow.

CASE 19
The Marathon:
On the meaning of a public event

This case study reports on a project at Eindhoven University of Technology in the Netherlands. The Designing Out Crime initiative within the university was asked by the City of Eindhoven to look into some issues relating to the marathon that is held in the city every autumn. After an extensive period of dialogue with stakeholders and other parties in the field, a two-hour frame creation workshop was held with the participation of the content specialist and seven designers.

1   ARCHAEOLOGY OF THE PROBLEM SITUATION

The Eindhoven marathon has been held since the early 1950s. It is popular with runners, and is known internationally as one of the faster circuits in the world. On marathon day, the main 42-kilometer full marathon run is accompanied by a half-marathon, a 10-kilometer run, and a kid's run—which all take place on parts of the same route. But the marathon is not very popular with Eindhoven residents. The marathon day is marked by many road closures, traffic diversions, and management of the very dense crowds. The local population tends to flee the city for that day. Those who stay feel frustrated, and tempers flare. Many people complain, and irate articles appear in the local press attacking the organization for the perceived mismanagement of the marathon. The city has already worked on improving communication about road closures and traffic diversions (using a website, ads in the newspapers, and a hotline), and more police have been applied to control the situation at specific problem sites. Still, dense crowds gather, mainly at the start and finish in the inner city, and getting around the city is hard on that day (especially if you have to cross the route). The traffic situation is perceived as chaotic and unclear. The City of Eindhoven has approached the Designing Out Crime initiative with this issue, which they define as a traffic control problem.

2   ESTABLISHING THE CORE PARADOX

After some discussion, the design team decided it had to step back from the traffic problem, as the city had already taken many reasonable measures to resolve it. What makes this problem situation difficult to tackle is the fact that the traffic problem might be a symptom of the way the marathon is managed and perceived.

Because the city of Eindhoven wants to be known in a positive light, it organizes a marathon.

Because of the marathon, streets need to be closed off.

Because streets are closed off, the inhabitants of Eindhoven tend to flee the city.

The semiparadox arises from this chain of reasoning: the first and third statement are not very well aligned.

3 THE CONTEXT

Next, the problem context is mapped, involving all stakeholders close to the problem situation. What are the goals and needs of this inner circle of stakeholders? What are their practices and what is their "currency"? First of all, the city of Eindhoven wants to be known as a serious cultural and social center, where things are happening. The marathon is seen as a good way to gain exposure, to put Eindhoven on the map. Simultaneously, the city council needs to convince the taxpayers of Eindhoven that their local taxes are well spent on something that is actually benefiting the city. Another key player is the city of Eindhoven itself, as a physical reality. Although it is the hub of a major high-tech industrial region, Eindhoven is a relatively small city to organize a marathon in. A large part of the route runs through suburbs that do not attract the marathon crowds. The international athletics body has a major regulatory influence on the circuit: start and finish have to be at the same location, and there are rules on gradients in the circuit, etc., to make the runners' times count in the world ranking. The foundation that organizes the Eindhoven marathon is very much aware of these rules, and has over the years developed a very fast circuit. The police want to have a safe and smooth-running event without incidents, with minimal police involvement. Local businesses in the center look forward to a busy day, with cafés and restaurants in the city center being the main beneficiaries.

4 THE FIELD

Outside the current problem context but within the broader problem arena, the participants of the frame creation workshop studied the people of Eindhoven, parents, children, schools, health insurance companies, shopkeepers in the suburbs, local citizens organizations, the bus company, the state railways, the organizers of other sporting events, the organizers of cultural events in the city, the University of Technology, companies large and small that have research labs in the Eindhoven region, the runners (choosing which marathon to run in the fall season), the runners' supporters, the ambulance services, the hospital, sponsors of the marathon, sponsors of individual runners, the suburbs themselves that might benefit from good media coverage, nature reserves outside the city, the region of East Brabant in which Eindhoven lies, etc.

The participants of the workshop discussed all of these groups thoroughly, in a discussion that gradually focused on (1) companies—they have a double interest in promoting a healthy lifestyle and attracting new staff who might consider Eindhoven as a good place to work; (2) the runners' families: they want to see their runner, and support him or her at a spot where it matters.

5   THEMES

For the city of Eindhoven, the marathon helps to fulfill an intense need for recognition, as it feels itself to be in competition with other cities. As an old industrial city, Eindhoven has not generally been perceived as a vibrant and interesting place to live. But this sense of competition that is so keenly felt by the city council is not shared by the general population, who really value this lively city for what it has, and do not mind that it is a well-kept secret. This is where the friction comes from—the traffic complaints, though grounded in reality, are a symptom of a broader pattern of public disengagement from the marathon. Meanwhile in the broader arena, there is a rich palate of cross-party themes that could help bring the marathon event closer to the needs of the city, merging with existing city concerns of workforce needs, inclusion of an increasingly varied population mix, relating the suburb and the city center, etc. The central theme that emerged from our discussions is that the marathon should be an appropriate fit for Eindhoven, showing the strengths and character of the city—but this can be achieved only through the inclusion of many more parties in the organization of the marathon day.

6   FRAMES

This theme sets us on a road from the current state of affairs (in which there is a marathon in Eindhoven) to creating a new event that truly and uniquely is "the marathon of Eindhoven"—an event that could not take place anywhere else because of the way it reflects and celebrates the character of this city. This means looking at opportunities to foster a sense of pride in what the city has to offer. Shifting the focus away from complaints leads us toward the creation of several frames. One approach to address this problematic situation is to give the marathon of Eindhoven to the people—to see the marathon as a self-propelled party (learning from the queen's birthday celebrations), with neighborhoods encouraged to organize events on that day. This process should occur from the bottom up, with local community organizations bidding for the honor to host part of the course.

If the marathon is approached *as if* it is a neighborhood event, *then* ...

Alternatively, the city of Eindhoven could provide the frame by dividing the marathon circuit into themed zones ("health," "design," "high-tech") in appropriate areas along the route—thus effectively seeing the marathon as a showcase for the city. Special events such as factory visits would draw the crowds away from exclusive concentration in the city center.

If the marathon is approached *as if* it is a showcase for the city, *then* ...

A third frame would be to make the marathon day less complex and intense by not combining all the runs, but instead holding the 10-kilometer and the kid's run over several weekends. Drawing out the events would add more of a sense of anticipation to the big race, and the marathon would be seen as one element of an initiative in health and well-being (the "Human Power Festival") in one of the top sporting regions in the country.

If the marathon is approached *as if* it is the culmination a "healthy city" season, *then* ...

On a completely different level, high-tech solutions could be developed to make the marathon route more permeable—e.g., sensors and lights alerting spectators of advancing runners. Mobile technologies could show onlookers the current position of "their" runner on the circuit, how he or she is doing relative to others, etc. Sophisticated high-tech solutions could be the hallmark of the Eindhoven marathon experience, an appropriate angle for what was named the top "smart region" in the world in 2011. This frame casts the marathon challenge as one of creating transparency and limiting the amount of friction within the city.

If the transparency of the marathon circuit is approached *as if* it is a problem of (social and physical) friction in public space ... , *then* ...

Please note that all of these framing metaphors are clear in themselves, but that the "patterns of relationships" that they suggest differ, that possible partner organizations in the solution space appear in various roles, and that the overall value created through these frames is not quite the same either.

7   FUTURES

In the development of design concepts and action scenarios based on these frames, we hope to find ways to combine several of these frames, integrating the needs of the widest possible group of people into a coherent solution. Space does not permit us to examine all of the scenarios that were developed in the course of the marathon project, but let's take the second frame, that of the "themed marathon," as an example. In pursuing this frame, the designers quickly discovered a hitherto hidden potential. They found that he marathon runners are mostly highly educated people, often on the technical side of the higher education spectrum, and that they come from all over Holland and Belgium (with a small number of people from other countries). In a region with high-tech companies that continuously need employees who fit this profile, this finding is significant. Having these marathon runners come to the city, many bringing along their families, thus creates a great opportunity to show off the region of East Brabant as a good place to live. The city could be very precise in orchestrating this appeal: by entering the runners' data in Google Street View, one could see the kinds of houses where these people live now, and then use the information to organize events along the marathon route that would expose visitors to the possibility of a lifestyle in the Eindhoven region that they will be most likely to enjoy. International recruitment could be galvanized by extending publicity for the Eindhoven marathon into Germany and other neighboring countries. It could be an attractive business proposition for the local companies to become involved in the marathon, adopt a theme along part of the marathon route, and properly show what the city has to offer. Including businesses would, in turn, involve more of the Eindhoven population in the marathon day. ... This is just one path of inquiry; there are many more. Please note that even in all the far-flung directions that the four frames might lead us, there is a bottom line: the original problem of the traffic complaints. All solutions will have to address that point—either by reducing the alienation of the population, by dispersing the marathon crowds in time or in space (as with the themed sections of the city; see figure 8.1), or by creating a more permeable circuit.

8   TRANSFORMATION

The next step is one of (creative) deduction: taking the idea of the themed marathon circuit, we map out the support structures that need to be further developed and implemented, and then outline the changes that would be required

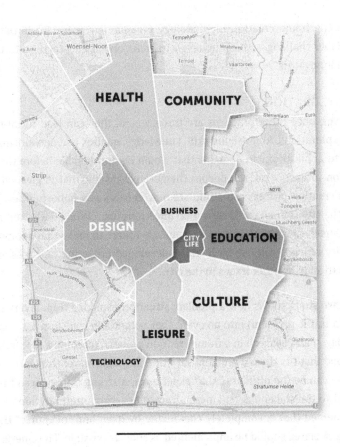

Figure 8.1
The Eindhoven Marathon: city themes and their location (based on a proposal by TU
Eindhoven students).

in the practices of those individuals and organizations involved. In this case,
companies and institutions in a specific sector (high-tech, design, health, etc.)
will be required to work together in a sensitive area like recruitment. That may
or may not be feasible in all theme sectors, and alternative scenarios might
need to be developed. City officials will find themselves in the role of facili-
tator/mediator, and be asked to develop the new rules for this new function.

While the frame creation methodology creates new space for initiatives, it invariably challenges those involved to transform their practices to become frame innovators.

9 INTEGRATION

However, once these practices are transformed, they can lead to interesting new explorations. A newfound skill, knowledge, quality, and network may lend itself to applications in domains that would be unthinkable before the frame creation project. Also, the deeper theme-level insight that is gleaned in the frame creation process can stimulate new debates and opportunities. In this case, the city council could reflect on questions like, "Who do we want to compare ourselves with? How do we encourage others to make that comparison?" And city officials can use their newly developed brokering practices and networks to address other issues in the city.

This case study shows how a problem situation exploded from a very modest brief (a traffic problem) into an event that potentially transforms a whole city for a day. If all goes well in a frame creation process, reaching a new frame like this (one that fits the old problem situation like a glove, yet transforms it completely) can be the ultimate "Aha" experience. A strong frame doesn't need to be sold to the stakeholders: a new, all-encompassing interpretation of reality has emerged that is completely convincing by itself and "of course" the solutions associated should be implemented as soon as possible. The emergence of such a strong frame can make the whole frame creation process look like a film of a building demolition, but an explosion played backward: from a very messy cloud of dust arises a building where all the pieces fit together in a self-evident way. But that is the ideal case.

Over the years, we have also experienced the ways frame creation projects can falter and deliver less-than-brilliant outcomes. One such project concerned the redevelopment of a very complex public space in a city center. The problem was presented as one of urban planning, and thus was immediately framed as a spatial issue—bypassing the themes step almost completely, and leading straight into the generation of spatial solutions. Because the underlying themes were implicit, they were not strategically chosen to steer away from the current frames of the key stakeholders, and in the course of the ensuing process the solutions gradually gravitated toward fairly conventional outcomes. This situation was exacerbated by the fact that the partner organization we were working with was quite tangential to the core issues at hand, and had little influence. As a result, the scope of the project gradually collapsed to a tampering at the edges, rather than creating the bold new approach that the problem situation really required. While the project results were quite limited and were not advanced much further, some of the reframing ideas did shift the thinking of key stakeholders quite a bit—enough for them to pick up the project later and redo it based on these lessons learned. But overall, the project was very disappointing. We should have known better, but we got trapped in the perspective of our partner organization and reverted to early solution-focused thinking, and we never really escaped from its confines.

Examples like these do raise many pertinent questions. The first one, of course, is *when* to enter into a frame creation project: should we have accepted this one at all? In which situations does the frame creation approach work well, when is it problematic, and when is it almost impossible?

"RIPENESS"

When to do frame creation and when not? Designers tend to talk about this question in terms of the "ripeness" of a problem situation. From our experience, we have found that a situation is not ripe when the issue at hand is not really felt to be a problem by key people in the organization. Launching into frame creation becomes an uphill struggle when you first have to convince people that there *is* a problem—they have to at least intuitively feel that there is, even if that feeling is barely perceptible or not articulated. We have seen before that launching into frame creation is relatively easy when an organization is already confronted by the limitations of its own approach (even if this is just a feeling of unease or frustration). The city of Eindhoven is a nice example of that: they had already exhausted their own problem-solving capacity, yet the problem had not been resolved and pressure from the local media made the situation one that could not be ignored—so obviously a new approach was needed. And then we need to get the right people involved: we aim for the very top of the organization, not just because of their overview and span of control but also because it is much easier for them to think freely. Working with frame creation on the middle management level is always challenging, as the roles and tasks of middle management are defined within the conventional way of problem-solving in an organization. They cannot allow themselves to be pushed into a different way of thinking that goes beyond their current responsibilities. The good news is that in experimenting with frame creation over the last ten years, we have found that frame creation projects are often curiously strong and solid. They have an innate capacity to help unlock the analytical and creative capabilities of people as well as to harness the breadth of their life experience to achieve new frames. Being involved in frame creation and achieving recognition for your contributions in such an open and creative process is incredibly motivating and engenders a sense of personal growth and fulfillment. Often, frame creation projects take on a personal significance to people that goes far beyond their official scope. This is a classic win-win situation: organizations that can allow themselves to move beyond narrow conceptions of rationality and create practices that fully employ the abilities of all of their people will be all the richer for it.

"FRUITFULNESS"
While "ripeness" is the term that designers use to talk about problem situations, "fruitfulness" is the term they use when discussing solution directions. Like ripeness, this is a notion that needs some explanation. Fruitfulness is the sense that a certain frame will not be a dead end, but will lead to a rich "solution space" with interesting and viable ideas. In studying expert designers, one can observe them making split-second decisions on fruitfulness all the time; they seem to have a special sense for this. Making these judgments requires a broad experience in the field, of course; being able to look into the future and prejudge situations and solution directions is almost the definition of expertise. The expert's ability to make split-second judgments in these processes is in marked contrast to less experienced participants, who will have to follow a solution direction until they get stuck, backtrack, and start all over again if it doesn't work. Thus, they laboriously build up the capacity to judge fruitfulness over the course of many projects. There are no shortcuts to achieving the magical ability to judge fruitfulness: at this point we reach the limit of what a method like frame creation can do. Methods are merely explicit patterns of practice, in this case based on the ways that real experts work. By making experts' patterns of practice more explicit, we seek to help nonexperts in a field to also reach a good result. Going through a considered pattern of steps or phases can help them avoid some pitfalls and can make a process more manageable—but this handy sequence of steps can never replace true expertise. So there are a couple of points in the frame creation methodology (around the high-level notions of "ripeness" and "fruitfulness" and, as we will see, around the strategic choice of the "right" themes) where experience and expertise really make a difference. In

our own practice, these are the moments when we make sure high-level experts are involved to guide the process along.

CHOOSING THE "RIGHT" THEMES

Choosing the "right" themes is a difficult step in the frame creation process, and a highly strategic one: through the choice of themes and the selection of concepts "to think with," one is generating frames that are pertinent to the themes. The trick is that the themes chosen should not be too literal or too close to the themes and frames that underlie current solutions. Also, when the several themes chosen are all combined, they should still be centered around the core and salient aspects of the original problem brief. Choosing themes one-sidedly can pull the whole frame creation process off course by creating undue emphasis on one part of the problem arena. In the marathon example, the themes of "recognition," "appropriateness," and "inclusiveness" can be seen as portraying the entire problem arena on a deeper, fundamental level. In practice, it may take a lot of creative thought and quite a number of iterations to select the themes that are "right," in that they are balanced as a set and together spark the development of a truly valuable new approach to the problem situation. These iterations are important and inevitable, and will have to be tolerated: taking the steps to develop themes and, from there, to develop frames is crucial in the frame creation approach; more than any other part of the process, this determines the quality of the outcome. In a way, it should not surprise us that these steps are hard. Fundamentally, frame creation is a design-based practice that was developed from the working methods of expert designers. By making their frame creation approaches explicit and accessible, we haven't made them any easier. But the strength of the frame creation model lies in the fact that less experienced teams can also get really good results through the thoughtful application of the processes, principles, and practices outlined in this book.

FROM CONTEXT TO FRAMES

As we've seen, within the frame creation approach themes emerge from the correspondence of deeper meaning and value among the players in the broad problem field. The identification of such themes can be achieved through the filtering processes that have been developed within the context of hermeneutic phenomenology (see chapter 3). A reasonably quick and dirty way to advance this process of emergence is illustrated in figure 8.2. One can start a matrix by making a list of the core stakeholders (from the "context" step of the process) and the players in the "field" on the left side of a large piece of paper—steps (1) and (2) in figure 8.2. Then each of them should write down what is important to them: their needs, values, and "currency" on separate sticky notes (step (3) in figure 8.2). In the next step, these notes with the needs, values, and core currency concepts are reclustered into coherent groups (4), irrespective of the stakeholder or party in the field with which they were originally associated. In the process of labeling these clusters, or giving them a name, the possible themes emerge (5) that can be the core of nomological networks (6)—these are clouds of words that relate to the central concept in various ways, and together through these connections define that central concept; see figure 8.3. A thoughtful inquiry into these nomological networks then sparks the emergence of new frames (7).

THE STRENGTH OF A THEME

These themes then have to be thought through and analyzed. This step is tricky because themes are complex constructs that contain psychological, social, and technical aspects, often in close connection. One way to formulate a strong sociopsychological theme is to consider the aspects of the human psyche: are there consistent and strong relationships between the emotional, cognitive, motivational, physical, social, and contextual dimensions of the theme in this particular problem situation? For instance, the theme of "identity forming" that seemed to play such a strong role for some of the groups of youngsters coming to the Kings Cross area can be understood in this way. The notion of social rank within a group of young males has all of these psychosocial aspects: the group is a high-pressure social environment that is tied to the deeply felt beliefs and values of its members—to what is considered "normal." It is also a highly emotional sphere, where the need to belong and the need to be seen as an individual with qualities of your own could easily clash with feelings of anger and frustration. The young men's personal goals in life are being shaped socially at a moment when the body is also going through great and unsettling

Figure 8.2
The frame creation workshop: a step-by-step approach to get from context to frames.

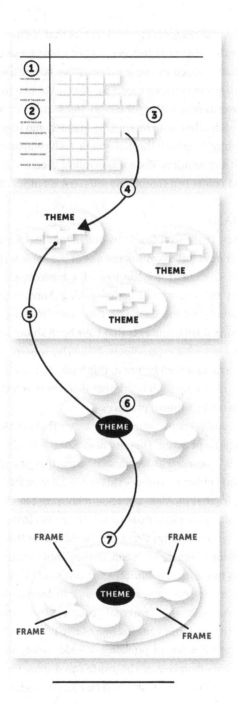

physical and biological changes. External factors that are part of an evening in Kings Cross can easily trigger aggressive or overly boisterous behavior, actions that are not actually caused by these externalities but by the way this theme plays out in such a group of young men. Likewise, in the marathon example, the themes of appropriateness (fitting the city) and inclusiveness (involving the city) strengthen each other in an interesting manner, and together frame possible actions by highlighting both the major high-tech companies and citizens as the key players in any solution. The sociotechnical theme of friction highlights a key variable and points in a completely different set of solution directions.

THEMES TO FRAMES

In chapter 5 we saw that to get from this understanding of a theme to the creation of possible frames (often considered one of the hardest steps in the frame creation process), one could use the tool of a nomological network, which effectively creates an in-between step. In making a nomological network, we put the central concept of the theme (in this case: "forming identity") in the middle and surround it with concepts that have been shown in earlier research to have a relationship with it (see figure 8.3). (The concept of a nomological network has, in fact, been used before in this book: figure 7.3 and its accompanying text form a nomological network that explicates aspects of novelty and its relationship to organizational practices.)

Next we strategically choose some of the terms that are close to the theme, and map the patterns of action that are associated with these terms. In this case, "strategically" means that we choose terms that are relevant, but in a nonobvious, slightly oblique manner—this is crucial in order to arrive at a new approach to the original problem situation (choosing too close to the theme probably means falling back into existing solutions). For instance, in the case of our group of young men at Kings Cross, one could look at the social position of the weaker/junior members in the group, as they are in danger of overcompensating their status by extreme behavior. As a pattern of behavior that might be useful in this regard, one could look at the way tribal societies ritualize, rather than regulate or suppress, these internal group conflicts. One could propose framing the situation in Kings Cross as one of ritualized conflict, and perhaps think as a solution direction of providing a wide variety of urban games or sports so that various members of the group can display their own particular physical or mental skill to the others and be recognized for it, thus releasing the social pressures on the weaker group members to assert themselves. Young

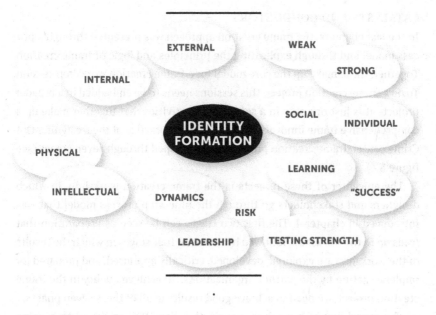

Figure 8.3
A nomological network for identity formation.

males are just one of the types that flock to the Kings Cross area on a Friday or Saturday night, and this is just one possible frame that could change their pattern of relationships and behavior. In frame creation, we create many of these frames, so we see whether and how they can be creatively combined: if frames lead to action patterns that are close or matching, and to solution directions that overlap, they become more interesting as contributions to an overall solution. Then a dominant concept can emerge that kills many birds with one stone. Say that in this case some of the urban game ideas would also relate well to other types of youngsters at Kings Cross (most importantly the girls), or be valuable as activities that could also be done during the day (by families); then they would emerge as more valuable and sensible options to pursue further.

CATALYSTS AND CONDUCTORS

In the last chapters, the frame creation approach was presented through a process model and through explicating the principles and logic of frame creation. Together, these make up the core model for a frame creation workshop session. To do a frame creation project, this sessions needs to be embedded in a broader project—it is just one step in a sequence of activities that together make up a comprehensive frame innovation process. In the practice of the Designing Out Crime center, frame creation projects are developed through seven stages (see figure 8.4).

The epicenter of these projects is the frame creation workshop, in which designers and stakeholders go through the nine-step process model that was introduced in chapter 4. The first two stages can be seen as preparation that leads up to the workshop, followed by the latter four stages in which the results of the workshop are explored, developed, critically appraised, and prepared for implementation by the partner organizations. To achieve quality in the frame creation project, we need to achieve good results in all of these seven phases.

The stated aim of a catalyst organization like DOC or YD/ is to become (largely) expendable by developing frame innovation capacity in its partner organizations. This is a complex task, as the different steps in frame creation involve quite different practices that are each built upon specific abilities and skills, behind which sits a particular creative "mentality." All the different activities need to be strung together in a coherent process for the thing to work. The catalyst organizations that we have looked at in this book are both doing this in their own way, and they are also themselves changing over time: the Young Designers foundation has turned from being project-focused (see cases 5 and 6) toward creating environments for transdisciplinary exchange (case 7), and then toward taking a theme-based approach (case 16). The Designing Out Crime center is in a completely different position, as it is based in academia (at the University of Technology, Sydney, and at Eindhoven University of Technology). This position is reflected in its working processes. Within the DOC project model (see figure 8.4), the core staff and postgraduate students concentrate on the earlier phases of the frame creation process (up to and including the proposing of new frames), while undergraduate students explore these new futures in many different directions. Experience has shown that if the framing has been done well, all the solutions that the undergraduate students generate will be interesting and useful. The center's staff and professional associates then take these ideas to a professional level for the handover to partner organizations.

RESEARCH

GATHER KNOWLEDGE REQUIRED TO TACKLE A
PROBLEM SITUATION AND IDENTIFY STAKEHOLDERS

v

INITIATION

KEY STAKEHOLDERS ARE CONTACTED
AND THE PROJECT IS FORMED

v

FRAME CREATION

NINE-STEP FRAME CREATION WORKSHOP (CH 4)

v

DESIGN EXPLORATION AND BUSINESS EXPLORATION

FRAME PROPOSALS ARE EXPLORED BY MAPPING OUT THE
DESIGN POSSIBILITIES AND EXPLORING THE (BUSINESS)
VALUE OF THESE DESIGN CONCEPTS AND IDEAS

v

PATH TO ACTION

MAPPING OUT THE ACTIVITIES AND THE
TRANSFORMATIONS NEEDED FOR REALIZATION

v

HANDOVER

RESULTS ARE HANDED OVER TO THE PARTNER
ORGANIZATIONS FOR IMPLEMENTATION

v

EVALUATION

RESULTS, PROCESS, AND UNDERLYING
METHODS/TOOLS ARE EVALUATED

Figure 8.4
Phases of a DOC frame creation project.

There are several benefits to this way of working: for the university, this is a good way to integrate research, education, and external engagement, while the frame creation process is helped enormously by the unbiased observations of the students. Working with young people who look at the world with fresh eyes is a crucial feature of both the Designing Out Crime center and the Young Designers foundation.

Apart from sparking changes in the ways that participating organizations work, frame creation can also spawn new networks of actors, and create new roles for organizations within these networks. In the marathon case study, for example, city officials take on a new role as network actor in the city. And indeed, in the aftermath of this small project, actor networks have come together and collaborations have led to first experiments to implement the proposed frames and solution directions. That this can be taken much further is proved in the Kings Cross case study (see case 17). The result is a confident new strategy called "OPEN Sydney—Future Directions for Sydney at Night," which sets out how the city seeks to become more "global, connected, diverse, inviting, and responsive." By entering into the process in this way, the City of Sydney as an organization has become an active agent in a completely new way. It has become a curator or perhaps even conductor of life in the city. It has not just reframed a problem, but has reinvented itself as a new actor within the city.

EMBRACING FRAME CREATION

Introducing the ability to create frames to an organization widens its repertoire of problem-solving strategies enormously, and deepens its knowledge of the outside world. When this is done successfully, something deeper and more lasting can happen. We have not yet focused our attention on the very last step of the frame creation process, "integration," but a small revolution can occur in this step from which a completely new type of organization is born. To understand this transformation, we have to look at organizations in a different way, beyond the problem-solving perspective we have maintained throughout this book, to consider frame creation as a structuring principle for organizations in and of itself.

In today's culture, networks of individuals form the basis for societal organization, in contrast to "mass societies" in which the collective organizes the individual. The historical uniqueness of this form can be contested—there have always been networks—but the scale and size of cooperation have grown enormously. (Van Dijk 1999, as quoted in Boutellier 2013)

This offers up an interesting perspective on organizations, in addition to the perspectives presented in chapter 6: a view of an organization as a set of overlapping and interacting frame innovators who jump into action when there is a problem (or opportunity), a perceived responsibility, and a possible "path to action" on the horizon. Within frame innovation, these "actors" are not the set organizational units that solve conventional problems; they are looser alliances that come together when action is needed and achievable.

METHOD CARDS

To support the steps of frame creation, the Designing Out Crime center in Sydney has developed a set of "method cards." Method cards were first introduced into the design discourse by the design firm IDEO (2003) as a way to convince their clients of their research credentials. IDEO created a set of fifty-two cards with brief descriptions on one side and an illustration on the flip side to explain the user-centered design methods and tools the firm uses. Having these tools on cards has proven to be a very useful in-house aid in setting up user-centered design projects: one can piece together a project from the different cards, even while in live conversation with a client. Within the firm, the cards ensure that whatever a designer or design team is doing, they are always "in a method," always applying a structured approach to activities that, without this type of gentle discipline, could descend into a vague and haphazard muddling around. The cards also emphasize that there are often multiple ways of executing an activity, and inspire triangulation on crucial parts of the development project. The IDEO method cards are publicly available, and although there is a temptation to adopt them wholesale and piece together a project by connecting the cards, one should be aware that they are in themselves an open-ended and nonsystematic set, based on the practices that were available in the firm at a moment in time. Also, the very brief descriptions on the cards stand for a lot of implicit professional knowledge in the organization. The best way to profit from the concept of method cards is to create your own set. Figure 8.5 offers a glimpse of some specific method cards supporting frame creation, which have been developed and used within the Designing Out Crime center.

The great advantage of a self-generated set of method cards is that it is situated (that is, relevant to the organization) and can easily refer back to salient aspects of common case studies. Each tool or method can be accompanied by the contact details of the person best suited to support its implementation, thus engendering both professional help in implementation and a sense of

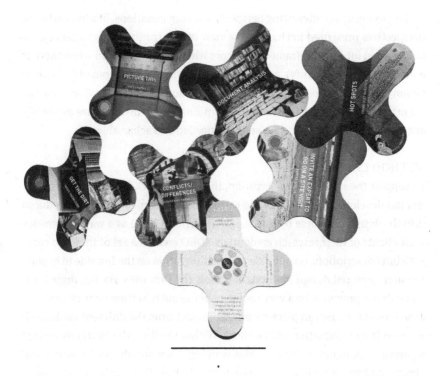

Figure 8.5
A sample of DOC method cards.

ownership and responsibility. Incidentally, the process of creating such a set of cards has a therapeutic quality in itself, giving each team member a sense of individual empowerment and creating an overview of how the different individuals contribute to the shared set of abilities and discourse. Making method cards helps establish the network of frame innovators mentioned above. The tools presented on the cards are often not new or original; their quality is to reflect existing practices and hopefully challenge people to extend them. Good sources of inspiration for the creation of such a set of tools abound in the design thinking literature; see, for instance, Brown (2009) and Martin (2009).

Common design and research tools used by designers can be found in Laurel (2003) and Kumar (2012).

Just as the set of frame creation method cards is open-ended, so is this book, which needs to start drawing to a close. Frame creation is a complex practice, and there are a million things still to impart to the reader at this point. These would include subjects such as the facilitation of the frame creation process, or the practice of "shadowing" a development project that is happening in a partner organization, using frame creation to show alternative paths and solutions in a live context. Or we might explore the conundrum of frame innovation and times of crisis: situations are often ripe for change when there is a crisis; but in a crisis situation, frame innovation might be perceived as too slow and cumbersome. There are also many things that frame creation still can't do, but might be able to once its practices have been developed further. Appendix 3 therefore briefly outlines a development agenda for frame creation and frame innovation.

PATH TO ACTION

What if many organizations adopted frame innovation as one of their core practices—what brave new world would that lead to? In sociological terms, the practice of frame creation would help organizations and people deal with a society that is less hierarchical and more fluid than ever before. This would result in a need to improvise; indeed, Boutellier (2013) has coined the phrase "improvising society" in his book of that name, where he explains:

Society no longer shapes itself around institutions; rather, the institutions must fold themselves around the events in an impulsive and fragmented society ... [society shapes itself around] a motif or "theme" that resonates and thus creates a sense of community.

But good improvisation (in the jazz sense) should always be based on a clear sense of direction and flow. These can be provided by the deeper layers of insight and structure that are built up in a frame creation process. The ubiquitous adoption of frame creation could lead to parties from different walks of life discovering that they are dealing with the same themes, and are creating frames that move in a similar direction. This could lead to interesting crossovers, shared practices, and shared projects and ventures. The rise of these new actors would be driven by people who have been described as "interpreters" (Verganti

2009) within a transdisciplinary process. A new type of network could result of people working together in communities where themes, frames, and ideas cross-pollinate and travel far and wide—driven not by the immediate necessity of a problem or need, but by engaging one another around a theme or frame.

At the beginning of this book, I posed the question of how individuals and organizations could deal with the open, complex, dynamic, and networked problem situations that characterize our age (figure 1.1). Through the study of advanced design practices and extensive experimentation, the frame creation approach was created and proposed as a possible answer. Interestingly, in frame creation, the open, complex, dynamic, and networked nature of problem situations is embraced and used as the path to solving them (figures 4.1 and 5.1). The problem is opened up through the analysis of the wider problem arena, and its complexity is increased by potentially involving a greater group of possible stakeholders. The dynamics of the problem situation are taken into account by the interactions that occur along the whole frame creation process, in analysis as well as in the creative steps (figure 5.2). This results in the agendas for transformation that support the resulting frames and solution directions. The networked nature of problems is an integral part of this broad approach, as it moves away from seeing only one "problem owner" and only one driver of the solutions. The depth and connection of the common themes and the shared understanding of the created frames produce a robust network of individuals and organizations to realize the new solution. Frame creation practices move quite freely and creatively within the complex problem arena between the rationalities that have contributed to the existence of the problem. Steering clear of these limiting rationalities (figure 7.2), and yet also avoiding the chaos of a random process, the frame creation approach provides a middle way toward the creation of a solution to the problem situation. Through the renewed framing of the problem situation, the root cause of the original issue is targeted. In a sense, this is more than problem-solving: it is the complete resolution of the problem. The ideal frame should resolve and eliminate the problem situation that gave rise to it, "and release the mind to do new things," to quote Wittgenstein. Interestingly, at the other end of the philosophical spectrum, the Indian philosopher Krishnamurti has said the same: "There is only the problem, there is no answer; for in the understanding of the problem lies its dissolution" (Krishnamurti 1995).

The power of this approach is beautifully exemplified in the following epilogue to the case study with which this book started in chapter 1, the impossible and fraught planning process for the high-speed train.

CASE 1
The high-speed train revisited:
All's well that ends well

We will now return to the high-speed train link and draw lessons from this classic drama, reporting a fascinating twist at the end of the project.

At the very last planning stage of the project, when the basic decision on the trajectory had been taken and approved in Parliament, scope remained for some changes to be made. The precise position of the tracks could still be tinkered with, a freedom of about 100 to 150 meters on either side. And every segment of the planned railway had been allotted a certain budget for ameliorating the impact of embedding the embankment in the landscape. Consultants were hired to lead discussions within the affected communities to determine how that money would best be spent. One of those consultants was dealing with a rural area, and was faced with the challenge of leading a workshop of about twenty very disgruntled farmers and their families. Picture a slightly nervous consultant in a local community hall, standing next to a whiteboard. In an attempt to clear the air and get a balanced view of the issues, he started by asking the group what was good about the high-speed train. A deep and long silence ensued, which was finally broken by the unwilling suggestion that it was probably good for the economy, and angry shouts about cutting travel time for *those* city people if they want to go to Paris. The next question after this slow start was, of course, what is bad about the high-speed train? This unleashed a barrage of comments that were duly written down. Then a map was brought out, showing the broad zone in which the train tracks had to be positioned. Gradually, the consultant mapped out the consequences of putting the tracks here or there. Crucially, the discussion veered away from its concentration on the problem of the train (see chapter 1) to a much broader discussion on the quality of life of people along the tracks. This is the conversation that should have been had fifteen years earlier, if only the process had been framed right: while a person's quality of life will be negatively impacted by the train, this can be compensated in other ways. For this agricultural community, working intensely with the land, the values that underpin their quality of life included a fundamental sense of ownership of the land that had sometimes been in their families for several generations. It was on the levels of practical problems and this shared outlook that fruitful discussions could be held. The

practical problems could mostly be overcome by compromise, often just split-
ting the inconvenience (OK, the tunnel is not ideally placed for me, but my
neighbors won't have to do a ridiculous drive to get to their land). The discussions that touched on deeper values were especially interesting. In one situation, the choice between alternative trajectories actually meant that one farm
or another would be completely eliminated. The initial stalemate was broken
when one of the farmers said that the other family had been there for much
longer than his, so he chose to leave. After all the conflict and strife that had
accompanied the entire high-speed rail project, this magnanimous gesture
was made from a profound sense of humanity. ... This is the moment to realize
that a badly run problem-solving process not only unnecessarily antagonizes
people but, by putting them on the defensive, forces them into a very narrow
behavior pattern. They can't be their nice, normal, and understanding selves
anymore because they are thrust into a position where they are forced to fight
for their immediate interests. This distances them from an essential part of
their humanity—in this case, for the many years of the project planning stage.
We have a moral obligation to do better, to devise problem-solving methods
that allow people to be themselves.

The development of frame creation from an approach to a model and eventually a full-blown methodology is very much a work in progress. There is no
better way to conclude this book than by inviting you to join in this exciting
venture. There is already a community working in this area, moving swiftly to
evolve the basic ideas that have been explicated in this book (see appendix 3).
Through the case studies, we have seen that the basic frame creation approach
can lead to results. The frame creation workshops are quite magical in their
ability to fundamentally shift the way people think, in only a couple of hours.
New patterns of meaning, structures for reasoning, and paths to action appear
where there were none before. This a fascinating and fun process that makes
problems disappear into thin air, and allows bright futures to emerge. Many
more of these projects should be done to help us understand the full potential
and significance of frame creation in different application areas.

I hope that the models and case studies in this book have given an impression of the frame creation approach. But there is a limit to what words can
achieve. I invite you to become a frame innovator and bring these insights,
models, processes, methods, and tools into action in your own environment.
This is important, as we face huge challenges in the coming years. Individuals

and organizations will increasingly be faced with open, complex, dynamic, and networked problem situations, and will have to adapt their problem-solving ability to cope. Developments like the growing inequality in the world, climate change, scarcity of resources, and environmental damage will generate myriad problem situations that just cannot be solved with our existing frames.

Wisdom is not only about knowledge and reflection; it is also about practice. At its core is the ability to do the right thing at the right time. Frame innovation alone is not the answer to all the challenges that individuals and organizations are going to face, but I hope the reader is convinced that there is wisdom in it.

APPENDIX 1: AN EXPERT DESIGNER AT WORK

My colleague Henri Christiaans and I studied individual designers working on a design task. The subjects were asked to think aloud so that their thought patterns could be captured and analyzed (this particular study was reported on in Dorst and Dijkhuis 1995; Dorst 1997). This particular series of protocol studies was performed with twelve experienced designers; the design challenge was to develop a new trash system for the passenger carriages of a new Dutch train. All the information needed to design a solution (e.g., background of the project, stakeholders involved, dimensions of the train, user research on the existing trains, etc.) was provided on information cards that the designers could request. The designers had 2.5 hours to tackle this design challenge. In this appendix we enter this protocol after an hour, during which the expert designer has been going through the information and discussing his own experiences with trash on the train and some comparable situations (trash collection in aircraft). Then suddenly, the designer jumps to an idea that might structure the problem situation for him.

(time: 60 min.) Just had a flash ... Would it be good to make separate bins? ... Because we have several different types of litter ... We've got the dry litter ... I would say paper bins ... Because lots of newspapers and magazines are left in trains ... I can imagine that you make a bin in which you can put newspapers and magazines, that kind of stuff ... That bin should be made in such a way that you can't put coffee cups and other stuff in there ... That's a problem ... Because people are bored ... That happens in trains ... They tend to start trying things that weren't supposed to happen ...

(time: 61 min.) But it would be a nice ... Well, there's a number of things crossing my mind now ... First, there's the railways ... The railways provide a mode of transport that is environmentally friendly ... That is still being used as an argument in favor ... And it would be a nice marketing ploy to expand that idea into litter collection ... With litter, I mean ... That the litter collection in trains could help that identity ... The environmentally friendly railways ... Then there would be in trains, where a lot of paper is thrown away, because that is the main kind of litter ... We could design the bins in such a way that we create a compartment where the newspapers can be put in ...

(time: 62 min.) So we ... I don't know how it will find its way in the rest of the litter processing ... But it would be nice if we could keep this paper separate from the rest of the litter ... Because that means that we have a bin that will not pose a number of problems in maintenance ... If I look at the current bin ... Then there is stench ... And it's too small ... It being too small is mainly because ... because it is full of newspapers and that kind of stuff ... It would be possible ... Because the newspapers are 40 percent if I remember ... Yes, 40 percent of the total litter is newspapers ... Almost half ... It would be so good to remove that beforehand ... It is dry litter ... It doesn't cause any visible dirt in the bins ...

(time: 63 min.) It isn't wet, or any of that ... It would be nice if we could make a simple compartment on the bin where people can just stick in their newspaper ... You don't use the bin as much ... You need less volume in the bin ... What was the mean filling ... 70 to 85 percent ... Of which 40 percent [is] newspapers ... That is an option anyhow ... To make such a newspaper bin ... And it has another advantage ... You see that newspapers and magazines are read by several passengers ... So if you don't put him in the same container with the coffee cups and the cans ... That the newspapers will remain clean ... And can be used again ...

(time: 64 min.) Now they stay on the table in the morning ... To leave them for the use of the next passenger ... I think the newspapers and magazines are also most of the stray litter ... I can't really tell from this information card ...

I think I heard that somewhere ... See if I can find it in the interview with Van Dalen ... Then it will probably ... Yes, the newspapers also block the emptying help ... They are a nuisance ... Lots of stray litter on the luggage racks ...

(time: 65 min.) What is on the luggage racks, ... As far as I know in trains, ... But now I'm only using my own experience ... There are newspapers and magazines on the racks ... I would like to start with the division between newspapers and other litter ... I'll put down that 40 percent of the litter is newspapers ... That means that the other bin can be smaller in size ... However wonderful ... That is an important thing ... I think it ...

(time: 66 min.) It is now at a height that is felt to be uncomfortable by everyone ... So we have to see whether we can find a better position ... Positioning ... For filling up and emptying, so to speak ... I think we have to try to get the bin as much against the wall as is possible. The trains are, as some people said ... Though not many ... Well, still, 8 percent ...

That bump their knees on the bins ... That's a nuisance ... If we can avoid that, we should ... So it would be nice to get the bin flatter against the wall ... And Mr. Van Dalen also said ... I think this has to do with his remark that he likes the integration of the bin in the wall so much ...

(time: 67 min.) You try to gain as much space as you can in the passenger compartment ... So let's say ... Has to stick out as little as possible ... Let's see ... Yes, and then there's stench ... And the filthy lid ... That filthy lid is brought up by almost 30 percent ... Yes, 28 ... We have to find something for that ... Important ... Then we have more problems ... That it is too small, of course ...

(time: 68 min.) This is also in my litter separation ... With the newspapers, etc. That includes the size ... Total size ... Then we have summarized in four points now ... The cleaners that would have to bend over so much ... Dark in the trains ... Too fast in flipping over ... That is the flipping over of the bins ... Sometimes ...

(time: 69 min.) The liquids in the bin splashes ... Turn over ... splashing of the liquids ... Yes, I'm putting it all together now ... Then you've got the newspapers ... OK ... I think that the separate collection of paper is all that's feasible ... Because other separations will be too complicated ... Do you know whether the railways are interested in the separation of litter in paper and other litter? ...

(time: 70 min.) That has not been discussed ... Yea ... But if I bring up the subject, can I then get an answer from the railways? ... In this way? ... EXPERIMENTER: You can raise the subject tomorrow ... Right ... And then we're presenting the concepts ... That means we'll have to work now ... I will look back to the current bin ... Because I want to see how far that sticks into the compartment ... The exact measures ...

(time: 71 min.) I don't think ... I'm making a drawing of the bin ... And I'm putting in the measures ... The total size of the product as it is ... Because I have some views here ... And I'm making a 3D sketch ... This is the height ... Section ...

And the lid ...

Interestingly, the separate bin is a solution that emerges as a possibly integrative frame idea from an intense analysis of the project brief and all the other information. These kinds of ideas have been called a "primary generator" in design, and they are to be taken as an initial frame that can lead to design ideas rather than as a core for a design concept. Taking this as a starting point, the designer retraces the value that can be achieved by this frame, and links it to the wishes of other stakeholders in the broader field—checking whether they would object, seeking to bolster the case for why this is a good solution direction, and seeking to enrich the frame with added value that might be achieved. This is an intense process of invention and reflection. The designer is carefully exploring an interpretation of the problem and a core solution idea together, in a close coevolution of the two. The paradox that gave rise to this quest was hidden in the brief:

Because the railway company wants to encourage use of the bins, the bins should be in easy reach for passenger comfort.

Because the railway company wants to encourage use of the bins, the bins should be quite big.

The paradox then becomes:

Because the bins are in easy reach for the passenger and quite big, they limit passenger comfort.

This is a classic problem for product designers: the product needs to be there and handy when in use, and not there when not in use (think of foldaway beds, inflatable mattresses, etc.). This need for the bin to "disappear" led other designers to come up with inventive placings of the bin, bins made of flexible material (to expand as they are filled), or the replacement of the bin by a chute (thus separating the functionalities of access and storage). This particular designer effectively chose to open the questioning by addressing the idea of what constitutes "rubbish," and explores putting newspapers separately. The themes he identifies that make this initial idea of separate bins valuable are the sense of being *environmentally friendly* (as a passenger, and as part of the image of the railway company) and that of *generosity*—leaving newspapers for the use of other passengers is a positive thing to do in a public space. The dominant frame in this episode is the separation of the newspapers from the other rubbish. This leads to the generation of a clear design brief: create a bin that is compact but has two separate compartments, one of which is designed in such a way that people will put only newspapers in it. In the evaluation of his initial design, he realizes that there is a second paradox in this problem situation:

Because the bins are in easy reach for the passenger, they are distributed throughout the cabin.

Because the bins are distributed throughout the cabin, they are hard to empty and clean.

This is where the needs of the passengers and the cleaners are at loggerheads (separate collection from multiple points makes life worse for the cleaners). In the end, this problem leads the designer to create a single, large newspaper rack at the end of the carriage, where passengers can leave their newspapers as they get off the train. This particular solution was graded highest of all twelve expert designs by a panel of independent judges. What will have struck the reader is that the designer seems to go more or less upside down and back to front through the design process. The process doesn't start with a problem definition, and the designer doesn't seem to have a structured way toward reaching a solution. And it also seems much messier than the clean, linear nine-step model of frame creation that was introduced in chapter 4. But if we take the initial idea as what it is—a frame idea that works as a "primary generator" guiding a possible interpretation of the problem situation—and we follow the twists and turns of the designer closely, it reads as a very coherent story. From this analysis, we find that expert designers tend to go through the steps of the frame creation process, but implicitly and fluidly. The elements of frame creation are there. In developing the frame creation method, we have straightened out these steps and brought them into a possibly logical order. But that is for modeling purposes—in reality, the steps will be executed in close interaction with one another, as the frame creators have to balance creative steps with analysis and reflection all the time. (This study later led to the Delft Protocols Workshop [Cross, Christiaans, and Dorst 1996].)

APPENDIX 2: IS DESIGN "SEARCHING" OR "LEARNING"?

The first paradigm through which researchers have studied and begun to understand design was introduced by Herbert Simon in the early 1970s (Simon 1973). In this paradigm, design is viewed as a rational search process: the design problem defines the "problem space" that has to be surveyed in search of a "satisficing" design solution. Seeing design as a rational problem-solving process entails adopting a positivistic view of science, taking natural sciences as the model for a science of design. The rational problem-solving approach to design is a combination of practice-based phase models of the design process and a model of the designer as an information processor from the field of cognitive psychology. The glue that holds these together is the theory of "human problem-solving." The central paradigm in this field is that problem-solving can be described as "a search for a solution through a vast maze of possibilities [within the problem space]. ... Successful problem solving involves searching the maze selectively and reducing it to manageable proportions" (Simon 1969, 54).

These search processes have been studied through protocol analysis of subjects solving chess and cryptarithmetic problems. They can be displayed and analyzed in "problem behavior graphs" (Newell and Simon 1972). Simon's key contribution to design methodology was to state that the productive design thought could be captured in the same positivistic framework. Problem solvers are seen as "goal-seeking information processing systems," operating in an objective and knowable reality. Simon explicitly states that his theory does not take into account the processes and results of human perception; it assumes that "human beings, viewed as behaving systems, are quite simple. The apparent complexity of our behavior over time is largely a reflection of the complexity of the environment in which we find ourselves." In studying an "adaptive system" (like man), we can often predict behavior from knowledge of the system's goals and its outer environment, with only minimal assumptions about the "inner environment" (Simon 1969, 53).

In a later paper, Simon (1973) addressed some of the difficulties that might arise in applying the rational problem-solving approach to design by defining design problems as "ill-structured problems." Ill-structured problems should be tackled in an "immediate problem space"—a part of the total problem space which is deemed too large, ill-structured, and ill-defined to be described. The immediate problem space is addressed and put together by an (unspecified) "noticing and evoking mechanism." The goal of a design process is to arrive at a solution that is "good enough": "we satisfice by looking for alternatives in such a way that we can generally find an acceptable one after only moderate search" (Simon 1973). In *The Sciences of the Artificial* (1969), Simon maintains that design problems are hierarchically organized, and the way to design a complex structure is to discover viable ways of decomposing it into subproblems, solving these, and combining them to arrive at a new overall solution. In problem-solving theory, a "good" (most efficient) reasoning process is defined as the one that involves the shortest search path through the problem space.

A radically different paradigm was proposed fifteen years later by Donald Schön (1983), who describes design as an activity involving "reflective practice." This pragmatist, constructionist theory is specifically made to address some of the shortcomings Schön perceived in the rational problem-solving approach to professional practice. Schön believes that the design component of the professions is underestimated, and that the nature of human design activities is misunderstood. Schön stresses the uniqueness of every problem situation, and identifies the core skill of designers as their ability to determine how every single problem should be approached. Schön calls this the essence, or "the artistry," of design practice, and finds it unacceptable that it cannot be described in the rational problem-solving framework.

To Schön, one of the basic problems for designers is to determine how to approach each single unique task through "a kind of knowing [that] is inherent in intelligent action" (Schön 1983, 50). Although he recognizes that this implicit "knowing-in-action" is difficult to describe and convey to students, he argues that what can be taught and considered is the explicit reflection that guides the development of one's knowing-in-action habits. This he calls "reflection-in-action." In a "reflective conversation with the situation," designers work by *naming* the relevant factors in the situation, *framing* a problem, making *moves* toward a solution, and *evaluating* those moves. The frames are based on an underlying background theory that corresponds with the design-er's view of design problems and his or her personal goals. Schön contrasts this theory with the positivistic rational problem-solving approach, remarking that "although Simon proposes to fill the gap between natural sciences and design practice with a science of design, his science can be applied only to well-formed problems already extracted from situations of practice" (47).

The description of design as a reflective conversation concentrates on the structuring role of the designer, setting the task and outlining possible solutions all in one framing action. The strength of this framing action determines the amount of structure in the task The central concept of *framing* was taken into the realm of organizations by Chris Argyris, who stressed the learning cycles ("single loop" and "double loop") in which framing takes a crucial role (Argyris 1992). These ideas have progressed in the work of Senge and others, emphasiz-ing the importance of the "learning organization" (Senge 2006). Many people immediately recognize these theories as a description of an important aspect of the organizational lifeworld. But they have also been criticized as lacking the kind of structure that one needs to run an organization—the kind of structure that rational problem-solving seems to provide. The rational problem-solving methods start out with goal definition and build an extensive apparatus of planning and control methods to achieve this preconceived goal in the most efficient manner. This allows for structured working processes that can be con-trolled unequivocally and measured objectively.

The two paradigms established by Simon and Schön are representations of two fundamentally different ways of looking at the world—positivism and con-structionism—and as such they are on opposite sides of a deep schism that runs through science and philosophy. They both have a role in understanding design practices (Dorst 1997).

APPENDIX 3: MORE RESEARCH IS NEEDED

The development of frame creation from the level of a proof of concept for a core process model to a true design-based methodology that can be applied in organizations is a daunting task, because a methodology sits between the worlds of academic discussion and real-world practice. Thus, it should be assessed on criteria that range from internal coherence and integration to external validity (for the proposed application area), but at the same time it should also be practical. "Practicality" means that the methodology should be actionable and work within the constraints of practice, be applicable with relative ease, be effective (do what it promises), and be efficient (deliver this in a timely and resource-lean manner). Not only should it be internally consistent (free of inner contradictions) on a theoretical level, but it should not lead to absurdities or morally unacceptable outcomes in the real world. For a methodology to be taken up in practice, it is important for it to be perceived as useful relative to contemporary challenges and a valid way of approaching these challenges. Academic standards, on the other hand, require that a methodology have some novelty relative to the academic discussion—that is, it should further the discussion in the field of research and spawn new, fruitful avenues of research. To deliver on the academic criteria, the methodology must have explicit and clear assumptions, goal, and scope, and the nature and scope of its contribution to the field must be carefully articulated. In a mature academic field like design research, we expect a methodology to be both theoretically and empirically grounded. We seek to achieve this formidable balancing act by placing the frame creation methodology development program squarely between academia and practice, and building it up in steps that generate academic, methodological, and real-world innovations along the way.

At the end of every academic paper, the author tries to convince the reader that "more research (and funding) is needed." In this case, it is true: while we have learned a lot about frame creation, there is much more to discover. And several limitations of the frame creation approach to date need to be addressed: (1) The application of the frame creation methodology raises fundamental questions about the nature of the link between this type of "design" problem-solving and other types of problem-solving. (2) The current frame creation approach is based on observations of expert behavior from just two design fields (architecture and industrial design). Study of the practices of other design professions might lead to the discovery of other frame creation practices and methods. (3) The scope and variety of the problems that frame creation can deal with need to be explored. (4) If the goal of developing the frame creation methodology is to build up frame creation capacity in an organization (and reach true frame innovation), we need to create bridges into the academic fields of management, organization studies, and entrepreneurship.

These four critical questions outline the philosophical analysis, empirical studies, methodology development, critical experiments, and transdisciplinary embedding that are needed to develop the frame creation model to its full potential, and to further the broader frame innovation discourse.

APPENDIX 4: INSPIRATION

One of the inspiring features of frame creation is the fact that such an open approach uses the breadth of human qualities of individuals in organizations (see chapter 8). It has this capability because its deeper structure is built on an understanding of the repertoire of human approaches to the world, as it is structured in different cultures.

Various philosophers have ventured to approach the difference in cultures by delving into their "great books," anthropological studies, and literature to achieve a deeper understanding of the underlying drivers of a culture. Here we will use the framework presented by Mulder (1997) based on the work of Henri van Praag (1916–1988). Van Praag concludes that cultures generally fall into five fundamentally different value systems that he calls the "cultural codes": (1) shamanic, (2) Indian/Tibetan, (3) Chinese/Japanese, (4) revelation religions, and (5) Western scientific thought. Each of the five cultural codes in this typology represents a completely different set of values and a different orientation, a different way of giving meaning to the world and to human existence within it (Ford 2007). We will not be dealing here with the truth claims that are associated with these ways of making sense of the world; we will just be taking them as the basis for the metaphors people in the respective cultures tend to live by (Lakoff 1987).

Van Praag uses a simple figure (see figure 12.1) to outline the "settings" of the key relationships between Humanity, the Higher, and the World in these five different cultural codes. In general, the relationship between Humanity and the Higher is "belief," the relationship between the Higher and the World is "creation," and the relationship between Humanity and the World is "culture."

However, the shamanic tradition (1) makes none of these hard distinction between Humanity, the World, and the Higher that Western thinkers are used to. Life takes place in a state of constant creation (see the notion of "songlines"

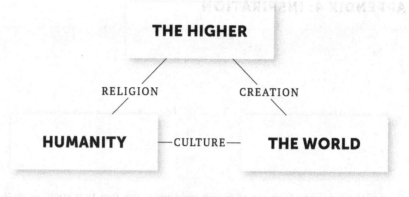

Figure 12.1
Humanity, the Higher, and the World.

within Australian indigenous cultures), within a *wholeness*. Because there is very little distance between humanity and the world, there is no room for Socratic questioning, as that is based on divisions (Ford 2007). The Indian/ Tibetan tradition (2) positions humanity and the world as having *layers* of consciousness. The goal of a human life then becomes to attain clearer consciousness and ultimately a complete connection in harmony with the world. The Chinese/Japanese tradition (3) also seeks harmony with the world, but in a different way: it sees the world as the dynamic operation of opposite forces (like yin-yang), where the attainment of *balance* is a key goal. The revelation religions (4) of Islam, Christianity, and Judaism see the connection with the Higher in the connection to a single God that can be addressed (prayed to) directly. In this way of thinking, humans are separated from God—the relationship with God and the world is a *transactional* one, in which prayer and morally good behavior are rewarded by God's love and a place in heaven. In Western scientific thought (5), the existence of the Higher is seen as a question of personal preference, and humanity is separated from the world. The world is a subject of objective study through the application of reason, for the attainment of understanding and truth. This is a *mechanistic* view of the world and human existence. The overwhelming emphasis on control, combined with a mechanistic worldview, easily leads to an exploitative relationship to the natural world and indeed to fellow humans.

To illustrate the way these different cultural codes work out in practice, we could take the example of the medical profession: issues of sickness and death are a universal human concern, and all cultures have developed a way to deal with them. Not only do the different codes have widely different way of dealing with sickness, they also have widely different concepts of what a doctor is. The role and methods of working of the shamans, Indian medicine, Chinese medicine, and Western medical practice could hardly be more different.

The openness of the frame creation approach extends beyond the confines of Western thought—in a way, frame creation invites us to use all thinking patterns that we can humanly muster to create solutions to bafflingly complex problem situations. And the different "cultural codes" have much to offer, both in their methods and in their ability to give words to phenomena that have been left without description in the dominant cultural code, which is a combination of the revelation religions and Western scientific thought.

The Japanese cultural code, with its attention to balance, has given us both the fine sensitivity of the Japanese aesthetic (Tanizaki 1977) and the cool-blooded balance of Musashi's book on strategy written in 1645 (Musashi 1974). For the practice of frame creation, the Japanese form of poetry called *renku* is particularly relevant, as it introduces a very special kind of reframing. In renku, overlapping verses of poetry are written by a group of poets taking turns. The poet whose turn it is takes the last two or three lines of the verse before and adds three (or two, respectively) in such a way that the meaning of the original lines is reframed. The process is led by the renku master, who imposes strict rules on the nature of the reframe: e.g., that the "rhythm" or "energy" should be constant while reversing the subject, or that a formal aspect should be played on while expanding the scope of the imagery. Matsuo Bashō (1644–1694) is considered to be the greatest renku master that ever lived (Ueda 1982). The ancient art of renku thus gives us a subtle vocabulary for framing and reframing, the playful changing of points of view that is considered to be a core design ability. This approach is significant because in the West, framing and reframing are often treated as "creative"—as just "random" processes—effectively dismissing these impressive leaps of thought as beyond reason and therefore unfathomable. Careful study of the language of the renku master helps us understand this crucial design skill on a much deeper level.

In Hindu philosophy, a deeper understanding of the world is achieved through connecting to a series of levels of meaning. This is a strong personal inspiration for me, as it is connected to my yoga practice in the Dru yoga tradition. Inadvertently and inevitably, this book contains many layered models of design and its relationship with the world. A direct link to the practice of frame creation can be found in the Indian notion of the koshas. The koshas describe five distinct layers of potential human involvement in action, which can be used as a map of how we as humans relate to the world and act in it: (1) First is the physical layer, which concerns our actions, physical reality, and our awareness of these facts. (2) The second layer deals with notions of energy and flow, and also where we direct our energy (the impetus for action). (3) The third layer describes how we relate to the world, and involves the emotions. (4) Fourth is the layer of intellectual understanding, thoughts, and convictions. (5) Layer five holds the deeply felt connection to the larger world, and is experienced as a sense of peace and stillness. Interestingly, this fifth layer is not seen as a goal in itself: within the Hindu tradition, wisdom is defined as being highly developed on all of these five levels. The frame creation approach strives to be complete in this sense too by considering action, impetus, emotion, discriminating thought, and broader learning in its steps.

REFERENCES

Argyris, C. 1992. *On Organizational Learning*. Oxford, UK: Blackwell.

Argyris, C. 2000. *Flawed Advice and the Management Trap*. Oxford, UK: Oxford University Press.

Bourdieu, P., et al. 1999. *The Weight of the World: Social Suffering in Contemporary Society*. Cambridge, UK: Polity Press.

Boutellier, H. 2013. *The Improvising Society: Social Order in a World without Boundaries*. The Hague: Eleven.

Bower, J. D., E. Crabtree, and W. Keogh. 1996. Rhetorics and Realities in New Product Development. In *Hidden versus Open Rules in Product Development*, ed. J. Thölke, G. Loosschilder, and F. Smulders. Delft: TU Delft Faculty of Industrial Design Engineering.

Brown, T. 2009. *Change by Design*. New York: HarperCollins.

Bucciarelli, L.L. 1994. *Designing Engineers*. Cambridge, MA: MIT Press.

Carlopio, J. 2010. *Strategy by Design*. New York: Palgrave Macmillan.

Cross, N. 2004. Expertise in Design: An Overview. *Design Studies* 25 (5):427–441.

Cross, N. 2007. *Designerly Ways of Knowing*. Basel: Birkhäuser.

Coles, A. 2012. *The Transdisciplinary Studio*. Berlin: Sternberg Press.

Cross, N. 1990. The Nature and Nurture of the Design Ability. *Design Studies* 11 (3):127–140.

Cross, N. 1996. *Method in Their Madness: Published Inaugural Lecture as Professor of Design Methodology*. Delft: Delft University Press.

Cross, N., H. Christiaans, and K. Dorst, eds. 1996. *Analysing Design Activity*. Chichester, UK: Wiley.

Deming, W. Edwards. 1993. *The New Economics for Industry, Government, Education*. Cambridge, MA: MIT Press.

Dickson, T. 2006. *Dansk Design*. Millers Point, Australia: Murdoch Books.

Van Dijk, J. 1999. *The Network Society*. London: Sage.

Dorst, K. 1997. *Describing Design: A Comparison of Paradigms*. Published PhD thesis, TU Delft, The Netherlands.

Dorst, K. 2002a. Hester van Eeghen: The Bag Is the Person (Hester van Eeghen—De tas is de mens). *Items* (May/June):64–71.

Dorst, K. 2002b. Orgacom: Art as a Reflection of Company Culture (Orgacom. Kunst als spiegel van bedrijfscultuur). *Items* (January):42–47.

Dorst, K. 2006. Design Problems and Design Paradoxes. *Design Issues* 22 (3):4–17.

Dorst, K. 2008. Design Research: A Revolution-Waiting-to-Happen. *Design Studies* 29 (1):4–11.

Dorst, K. 2011. The Core of "Design Thinking" and Its Application. *Design Studies* 32 (6):521–532.

Dorst, K. 2013a. *Academic Design*. Eindhoven: Eindhoven University of Technology.

Dorst, K. 2013b. Shaping the Design Research Revolution. Proceedings of the 19th International Conference on Engineering Design (ICED13), Seoul, Korea.

Dorst, K., and N. Cross. 2001. Creativity in the Design Process: Co-evolution of Problem-Solution. *Design Studies* 22 (5):425–437.

Dorst, K., and J. Dijkhuis. 1995. Comparing Paradigms for Describing Design Activity. *Design Studies* 16 (2):261–274.

Dorst, K., and D. Tomkin. 2011. Themes as Bridges between Problem and Solution. In *Diversity and Unity*, proceedings of IASDR2011, ed. N. Roozenburg, L.-L. Chen, and P. J. Stappers. Delft: Delft University of Technology.

Dreyfus, H. L. 1992. *What Computers Still Can't Do*. Cambridge, MA: MIT Press.

Dreyfus, H. L. 2002. Intelligence without Representation: Merleau-Ponty's Critique of Mental Representation. *Phenomenology and the Cognitive Sciences* 1:367–383.

Van Eeghen, H., and J. Gannij. 2009. *Bag and Shoe Design: Hester van Eeghen*. Amsterdam: BIS Publishers.

Ford, D. 2007. *The Search for Meaning*. Berkeley: University of California Press.

Foucault, M. 2002 [1969]. *The Archaeology of Knowledge*. London: Routledge.

Fukasawa, N. 2007. *Naoto Fukasawa*. New York: Phaidon.

Gamman, L. 2012. *Gone Shopping: The Story of Shirley Pitts, Queen of Thieves*. London: Bloomsbury Reader.

Gamman, L., A. Thorpe, E. Liparova, and M. Malpass. 2012. Hey Babe, Take a Walk on the Dark Side: Or, Why Role-Playing Is a Suitable Tool to Design against Crime and Aid Designers to Think Thief. *Design and Culture* 4 (2):171–193.

Gardner, H. 1983. *Frames of Mind: The Theory of Multiple Intelligences.* London: Heinemann.

Gardner, H. 2006. *Changing Minds.* Boston: Harvard Business School Press.

Graves, R. 1991. The Case for Xanthippe. In *The Oxford Book of Essays*, ed. J. Gross, 472–479. London: Oxford University Press.

Grenfell, M., ed. 2012. *Bourdieu: Key Concepts.* Stocksfield, UK: Acumen.

de Gruijter, M., E. Smits van Waesberge, and H. Boutellier. 2010. *Een vreemde in eigen land (A stranger in your own country).* Amsterdam: Askant.

Hanley, L. 2007. *Estates: An Intimate History.* London: Granta.

Hargardon, A., and R. I. Sutton. 2000. Building an Innovation Factory. *Harvard Business Review* (May–June): 157–166.

Harkema, C. 2012. *Revealing Unawareness in Usability-Related Decision Making.* Published PhD thesis, TU Eindhoven, The Netherlands.

Hart, S. 1996. New Product Success: Measurement, Methodology, Models, and Myths. In *Hidden versus Open Rules in Product Development*, ed. J. Thölke, G. Loosschilder, and F. Smulders. Delft: TU Delft Faculty of Industrial Design Engineering.

Hatchuel, A. 2002. Towards Design Theory and Expandable Rationality: The Unfinished Program of Herbert Simon. *Journal of Management and Governance* 5 (3):260–273.

Heat-Moon, W. L. 1999. *PrairyErth: A Deep Map.* Boston: Houghton Mifflin.

Heidegger, M. 1962. *Being and Time.* New York: Harper and Row.

Hekkert, P., and M. B. van Dijk. 2011. *Vision in Design: A Guidebook for Innovators.* Amsterdam: BIS Publishers.

Heskett, J. 1985. *Industrial Design.* London: Thames and Hudson.

Hirshberg, J. 1998. *The Creative Priority.* New York: Harper Business.

Hofstadter, D. 1979. *Gödel, Escher, Bach: An Eternal Golden Braid.* London: Penguin.

Hofstede, G. 1997. *Cultures and Organizations: Software of the Mind.* New York: McGraw-Hill.

Hofstede, G. 2001. *Culture's Consequences: Comparing Values, Behaviors, Institutions, and Organizations across Nations.* Thousand Oaks, CA: Sage Publications.

Houkes, W. N., P. E. Vermaas, K. Dorst, and M. J. de Vries. 2002. Design and Use as Plans: An Action-Theoretical Account. *Design Studies* 23 (3):303–320.

IDEO. 2003. *Method Cards: 51 Ways to Inspire Design*. Palo Alto, CA: IDEO.

Jacobsen, M. H., ed. 2009. *Encountering the Everyday: An Introduction to the Sociologies of the Unnoticed*. New York: Palgrave Macmillan.

Krishnamurti, J. 1995. *The Book of Life*. New York: Harper One.

Kroes, P., M. Franssen, and L. Bucciarelli. 2009. Rationality in Design. In *Philosophy of Technology and Engineering Science*, ed. A. W. M. Meijers. Amsterdam: Elsevier.

Kuhn, T. S. 1962. *The Structure of Scientific Revolutions*. Chicago: University of Chicago Press.

Kumar, V. 2012. *101 Design Methods: A Structured Approach for Driving Innovation in Your Organization*. Chichester, UK: Wiley.

Lakoff, G. 1987. *Women, Fire, and Dangerous Things: What Categories Reveal about the Mind*. Chicago: University of Chicago Press.

Lakoff, G., and M. Johnson. 1980. *Metaphors We Live By*. Chicago: University of Chicago Press.

Lakoff, G., and M. Johnson. 1999. *Philosophy in the Flesh: The Embodied Mind and Its Challenge to Western Thought*. New York: Basic Books.

Latour, B. 1987. *Science in Action*. Cambridge, MA: Harvard University Press.

Laurel, B., ed. 2003. *Design Research: Methods and Perspectives*. Cambridge, MA: MIT Press.

Lawson, B. 1994. *Design in Mind*. Oxford, UK: Butterworth-Heinemann.

Lawson, B., and K. Dorst. 2009. *Design Expertise*. Oxford, UK: Architectural Press.

Lawson, H. 2001. *Closure: A Story of Everything*. London: Routledge.

Leadbeater, C. 2001. *Living on Thin Air: The New Economy with a New Blueprint for the Twenty-first Century*. London: Penguin.

Lefebvre, H. 2008. *Critique of Everyday Life*. Vol. 2. New York: Verso.

Le Roy Ladurie, E. 1979. *Carnival in Romans*. New York: George Braziller.

van der Lugt, R. 2001. *Sketching in Design Idea Generation Meetings*. Published PhD thesis, TU Delft, The Netherlands.

Maher, M. L., J. Poon, and S. Boulanger. 1996. Formalising Design Exploration as Co-evolution: A Combined Gene Approach. In *Advances in Formal Design Methods for CAD*, ed. J. S. Gero and F. Sudweeks. London: Chapman and Hall.

van Manen, M. 1990. *Researching Lived Experience*. Ontario, Canada: Althouse Press.

Martin, R. 2009. *The Design of Business*. Cambridge, MA: Harvard Business Press.

Morgan, G. 1986. *Images of Organization*. Thousand Oaks, CA: Sage Publications.

Mulder, B. 1997. *Unpublished Lecture Notes on Cultural Codes*. Utrecht, The Netherlands: Lectures for the Parapsychology Institute.

Musashi, M. 1974. *A Book of Five Rings*. Woodstock, NY: Overlook Press.

Newell, A., and H. A. Simon. 1972. *Human Problem Solving*. Englewood Cliffs, NJ: Prentice-Hall.

Norman, D. 2010. Why Design Education Must Change. *Core77*, November 26, http://www.core77.com/blog/columns/why_design_education_must_change_17993.asp.

Pappers, D., J. Kolkman, P. Suyling, and J. Engel, eds. 1999. *YD+I—Young Designers and Industry 99, Minds over Matter—31 Designers Work with 9 Companies*. Amsterdam: Sandberg Institute and the Netherlands Design Institute.

Paton, B., and K. Dorst. 2011. Briefing and Reframing: A Situated Practice. *Design Studies* 32 (6):573–587.

Plattner, H., C. Meinel, and U. Weinberg. 2009. *Design Thinking—Innovation lernen—Ideenwelten öffnen*. Munich: Mi-Wirtschaftsbuch, Finanzbuch Verlag GmbH.

Priemus, H. 2009. Besluitvorming over megaprojecten (Decision making in mega-projects). In *Rijdende treinen en gepasseerde stations*, ed. J. de Vries and P. Bordewijk. Amsterdam: Van Gennep.

Roozenburg, N. F. M., and J. Eekels. 1995. *Product Design: Fundamentals and Methods*. Chichester, UK: Wiley.

Sarasvathy, S. 2008. *Effectuation: Elements of Entrepreneurial Expertise*. Cheltenham, UK: Elgar.

Schön, D. A. 1983. *The Reflective Practitioner: How Professionals Think in Action*. London: Temple Smith.

Schön, D. A. 1987. *Educating the Reflective Practitioner*. San Francisco: Wiley.

Senge, P. M. 2006. *The Fifth Discipline: The Art and Practice of the Learning Organization*. New York: Random House.

Simon, H. A. 1969. *The Sciences of the Artificial*. Cambridge, MA: MIT Press. 2nd ed. 1982.

Simon, H. A. 1973. The Structure of Ill-Structured Problems. *Artificial Intelligence* 4: 181–201. Rpt. in *Developments in Design Methodology*, ed. N. G. Cross. Chichester, UK: Wiley, 1984.

Smulders, F. E. H. M. 2006. *Get Synchronized: Bridging the Gap between Design and Volume Production*. Published PhD thesis, TU Delft, The Netherlands.

Stacey, R., D. Griffin, and P. Shaw, eds. 2000. *Complexity and Management: Fad or Radical Challenge to Systems Thinking?* London: Routledge.

Stacey, R., D. Griffin, and P. Shaw, eds. 2006. *Complexity and the Experience of Managing in Public Sector Organizations*. New York: Routledge.

Steyaert, C. 2007. Entrepreneuring as a Conceptual Attractor? A Review of Process Theories in Twenty Years of Entrepreneurship Studies. *Entrepreneurship and Regional Development* 19 (November).

Suchman, L. A. 1987. *Plans and Situated Actions*. Cambridge, UK: Cambridge University Press.

Sutton, R. I., and A. Hargardon. 1996. Brainstorming Groups in Context: Effectiveness in a Product Design Firm. *Administrative Science Quarterly* 41:685–718.

Sutton, R. I., and T. A. Kelley. 1997. Creativity Doesn't Require Isolation: Why Product Designers Bring Visitors "Backstage." *California Management Review* 40 (1):75–91.

Suyling, P., D. Krabbendam, and K. Dorst, eds. 2005. *More Than Eight Design Ideas for the Integrated Living of Mentally Handicapped People in Society*. The Hague: Ministry of Health, Wellbeing, and Sports.

Tanizaki, J. 1977. *In Praise of Shadows*. New Haven, CT: Leete's Island Books.

Thorpe, A., and L. Gamman. 2011. Design with Society: Why Socially Responsive Design Is Good Enough. *CoDesign* 7 (3–4):217–230.

Tzonis, A. 1992. Huts, Ships, and Bottle Racks: Design by Analogy for Architects and/or Machines. In *Research in Design Thinking*, ed. N. Cross, K. Dorst, and N. Roozenburg. Delft: Delft University Press.

Ueda, M. 1982. *The Master Haiku Poet Matsuo Bashō*. Tokyo: Kodansha International.

Valkenburg, R. 2000. *The Reflective Practice in Product Design Teams*. Published PhD thesis, TU Delft, The Netherlands.

Valkenburg, R., and K. Dorst. 1998. The Reflective Practice of Design Teams. *Design Studies* 19 (3):249–271.

Verganti, R. 2009. *Design-Driven Innovation*. Boston: Harvard Business School Press.

de Vries, J., and P. Bordewijk. 2009. *Rijdende treinen en gepasseerde stations* [The train has left the station]. Amsterdam: Van Gennep.

van de Wetering, J. W. 1999. *The Empty Mirror: Experiences in a Japanese Zen Monastery*. New York: Thomas Dunne Books.

Whitbeck, C. 1998. *Ethics in Engineering Practice and Research*. Cambridge, UK: Cambridge University Press.

Winograd, T., and F. Flores. 1986. *Understanding Computers and Cognition*. Norwood, NJ: Ablex Publishing.

Wittgenstein, L. 1963. *Philosophical Investigations*. Oxford, UK: Blackwell.

Zeldin, T. 1994. *An Intimate History of Humanity*. New York: HarperCollins.

Van Zomeren, K. 2000. *Ruim duizend dagen werk*. Amsterdam: De Arbeiderspers.

INDEX

Abduction, 48

Academic design, 129

Aloneness, 119

Amsterdam Historic Museum, 20

Archaeology, 74

Argyris, Chris, 185

Bang and Olufsen, 5–7, 121–122

Bashō, Matsuo, 191

Behavior, 39

Bourdieu, Pierre, 8, 76

Boutellier, Hans, 1, 18, 171

Brainstorming, 145

Briefing, 60, 107, 122

Business plan, 79

Business school, 147

Case studies

Bang and Olufsen, 5–7, 121

Circular Quay, Sydney, 34–35, 104

design school, 129–130

Eindhoven Marathon, 77, 151–158, 159, 161

employment services company, 23–24

high-speed train, Netherlands, 3–5, 138, 173–174

integrated living of mentally handi-capped people, 25–28, 52, 100, 102, 104, 136

Kings Cross, Sydney, 31–34, 45, 48, 54, 65, 106, 129, 134, 135, 162, 164, 165, 168

loneliness of mentally handicapped people, 117–120

shoplifting prevention, 36–37, 88–92

Smart Work Hubs, 110–114

social housing estate problems, 7–9

social housing, Sydney, 114–117

storytelling project, Amsterdam, 19–20

Stratums Eind, Eindhoven, 92–97

street fashion studio, Amsterdam, 29–30

Sydney nightlife, 128–129

Sydney Opera House podium, 80–87, 97, 103, 106

Catalyst, 128, 166

Christiaans, Henri, 74, 177, 181

Coevolution, 59

Conductor, 166

Context, 9, 54, 62, 76

Control, 28, 127

Crime prevention through environmental design, 39

Cross, Nigel, 43, 59, 74, 130, 181

Culture, 189

Deduction, 45

Design

abduction, 49

as creating beauty, 41

fixation, 61

good design, 44

and ideas, 42

Design (continued)
  misunderstanding, 41
  mysteriousness of, 43
  not irrational, 43
  as reasoning, 44
  strategic, 143
Design expertise model, 57–58
Designing
  practices, 55
  roles, 60
Designing Out Crime (DOC) research
    centers
  and Circular Quay, Sydney, 34–35, 104
  description, 30–31, 166, 169
  and Eindhoven Marathon, 77, 151–158,
    159, 161
  and Kings Cross, Sydney, 31–34, 45, 48,
    54, 65, 106, 129, 134, 135, 162, 164,
    165, 168
  and shoplifting prevention, 36–37,
    88–92
  and Smart Work Hubs, 110–114
  and social housing, 114–117
  and Stratums Eind, Eindhoven, 92–97
  and Sydney Opera House podium, 80–87,
    97, 103, 106
Design research, 43, 183
Design thinking, 2, 60, 170
Discourse, 42, 70, 79, 124
Dreyfus, Hubert L., 57, 138
Dutch Ministry of Health, Wellbeing, and
    Sports, 25, 26

Eeghen, Hester van, 68
Eekels, Johannes, 45
Effectuation, 148
Eindhoven
  Marathon, 77, 151–158, 159, 161
  Stratums Eind, 92–97
  University of Technology, 92, 151,
    153, 166
Entrepreneuring, 148
Evaluation, 55

Fashion, 29
Field, 76
Formulation, 55
Foucault, Michel, 42
Frame
  absorption, 125
  adoption, 124
  combination of, 165
  communication, 64
  definition, 63
  episodic nature, 65
  fruitfulness, 160
  and problem solving, 2
  quality, 64
  sharpness, 106
Frame creation
  model, 73, 120, 187
  practices, 109
  principles, 99
  process, 75
Frame innovation, 125, 126
Framing
  activity, 53, 78
  implicit, 136
Fukasawa, Naoto, 68
Futures, 78

Graves, Robert, 140

Harkema, Christelle, 74
Hart, Susan, 146
Heat-Moon, William Least, 20
Heidegger, Martin, 15, 140
Hermeneutics, 66
Heroism, 15, 147
High-speed trains, 3, 173
Home office, 62
Hyperconnectivity, 12
Hypothesis, 47

Idea, 42
Identity, 17
IDEO, 169

Implementation, 133
Improvisation, 141
Induction, 46
Industrial economy, 149
Innovation, 15, 143
Innovation management, 143, 148, 188
Integration, 59, 79
Intellectual capital, 71
Intuition, 54, 78

Johnson, Mark, 137

Knowledge economy, 149
Koan, 52
Koshas, 192
Krishnamurti, Jiddu, 172

Lakoff, George, 137
Lawson, Bryan, 42, 43, 57, 63
Leadership, 147
Loneliness, 117
Lone warrior, 13
Lugt, Remko van der, 74

MacCormac, Richard, 63
Management, 56
Manen, Max van, 66–67, 95
Marathons, 152
Meaning, 66
Mental institutions, 25
Metaphor, 32
Method cards, 169
Methodology, 160, 174, 187
Move, 55
Mulder, B., 189
Musashi, Miyamoto, 191
Music festivals, 32–33

Network society, 168
Nighttime economy, 129
Novelty, 144–149

Object worlds, 52
Open innovation, 146
Orgacom, 24, 25, 69
Organization
   continuity, 19
   culture, 17
   identity, 17
   learning organization, 185
Orwell, George, 18

Paradox, 50, 74
Paton, Bec, 74
Patterns, 104
Peirce, Charles Sanders, 45
Phenomenology, 66, 161
Planning process, 3
Postindustrial economy, 8
Praag, Henri van, 189
Practice, 130
   doing, 143
   seeing, 134
   thinking, 135
Pragmatist philosophy, 45
Primary generator, 59, 181
Private sector, 98, 148
Problem
   ill-structured, 184
   open, complex, dynamic, and networked,
      1, 9, 11–12, 126, 127
   resolution, 172
   space, 183
Problem situation, 12, 55
   ripeness, 159
Problem solving
   conventional, 49, 50, 124
   methods, 11–12
   problem definition, 12
   problem formulation, 13
Protocol analysis, 177
Public perception, 93
Public sector, 98, 148

Rationality, 16, 137, 142
Reflection in action, 184
Renku, 191
Representation, 55
Retail, 7, 88
Risk, 94, 147
Roozenburg, Norbert, 45
Routine, 122

Schön, Donald, 184–185
Senge, Peter M., 185
Sherlock Holmes, 18, 47
Shoplifting, 36, 88
Simon, Herbert, 183–184, 185
Simplification, 103
Skunk works, 146
Slob, Miriam, 27
Smulders, Frido, 74
Social housing, 7–9, 19–20, 114
Solution space, 183
Storytelling, 20
Success, 146
SWOT analysis, 145
Sydney
    Circular Quay, 34–35, 104
    Kings Cross, 31–34, 45, 48, 54, 65, 106,
       129, 134, 135, 162, 164, 165, 168
    nightlife, strategic planning for,
       128–129
    social housing, 114–117
    Sydney Opera House podium, 80–87, 97,
       103, 106
    University of Technology, 31, 166

Tanizaki, Junichiro, 191
Theme
    analysis, 77
    definition, 66
    depth, 106
    nature, 67
    psychosocial, 162
    right, 161
    sociotechnical, 164
    strength, 162

Thinking outside the box, 16
Thrownness, 19, 140
Transdisciplinarity, 188
Transformation, 79

Urban sports, 164

Valkenburg, Rianne, 74
Vision in product design, 61

We Are Here, 29
Whitbeck, Caroline, 51
Wisdom, 175, 192
Wittgenstein, Ludwig, 60, 172

Yeang, Ken, 70
Young Designers foundation (YD/)
    description, 23, 166
    and employment services company,
       23–24
    and housing of mentally handicapped
       people, 25–28, 52, 100, 102, 104, 136
    and loneliness of mentally handicapped
       people, 117–120
    practice, 38, 168
    and street fashion studio, Amsterdam,
       29–30

Zeldin, Theodore, 67
Zomeren, Koos van, 140